Spiritual Leadership in the
Small Membership Church

Spiritual Leadership
in the Small Membership Church

DAVID CANADA

Abingdon Press
Nashville

SPIRITUAL LEADERSHIP IN THE SMALL MEMBERSHIP CHURCH

This book is printed on acid-free paper.

Library of Congress Cataloging-in-Publication Data

Canada, David, 1946–
    Spiritual leadership in the small membership church / David Canada.
        p. cm.—(Small membership church)
    ISBN 0-687-49482-6 (alk.paper)
    1. Christian leadership. 2. Small churches. I. Title. II. Series.

BV652.1.C39 2005
253—dc22

                                                                2005015021

05 06 07 08 09 10 11 12 13 14—10 9 8 7 6 5 4 3 2 1
MANUFACTURED IN THE UNITED STATES OF AMERICA

To
Judy, Mike, and Tina
My family and my inspiration

Contents

Contents

Acknowledgments

W orking on this book was a remarkable journey. It involved the support and prayers of many people. My wife, Judy, is always a source of the finest inspiration. Her love and kindness always seem to work miracles in my life and in the lives of all who know her. She inspired much of what is written here and also proofread the book as it was being prepared for publication. My son, Mike, and his fiancée, Tina, are both constant sources of joy and inspiration, and their encouragement kept me focused on the importance of this text.

All of my mentors made this book possible. The members of the churches I served have taught, challenged, inspired, and loved me. The members of the Burkeville United Methodist Charge have been especially helpful.

The clergy with whom I work have all made this work possible. I'm especially grateful to Bert Cloud for opening doors; to Sylvia Meadows, Callie Jackson, Rich Meiser, and Alexis Fathbruckner for encouraging me; to James Tongue, Rita Callis, and Godfrey Tate for being wonderful district superintendents and friends; and to the pastors of the Farmville District of the United Methodist Church for all the things they teach me every day.

I especially thank Terrie Livaudais, Kathy Armistead, Sarah Hasenmueller, and the other people at Abingdon Press for all their help and guidance.

Introduction

THE JOURNEY

The funeral home was packed with family and friends. Every member of Rocky Mount United Methodist Church was there to support the grieving widow. I was her pastor. I was twenty-five years old and had recently completed seminary. During a two-year appointment as a student pastor and a quarter of Clinical Pastoral Education (CPE) I was involved with the death and dying of many people. I felt pretty comfortable in the role of pastor to those experiencing grief.

Rocky Mount was a part of the Buckingham Charge, a three-church pastoral appointment in rural Virginia. Rocky Mount was the second oldest church in Buckingham County. It dated to the earliest days of Methodism in America. Many of the families in that church had been there since the beginning of the congregation. In many ways I was not yet comfortable with them. I did not know them as well as I wanted. I did not really feel like a part of the community. Yet I knew the role of a pastor in a time of grief. I knew how to offer appropriate pastoral care at the funeral home.

I stepped outside to get away from the crowd, and I heard two of the older women of the community talking about me. One of them said, "He's going to be a fine pastor someday." I felt crushed. All of the feelings I had about not belonging to the community came flooding into my consciousness. I wanted to duck my head and avoid looking at anybody. I was also frustrated. What about all the funerals I had conducted as a student pastor? What about all the deaths I had attended as a CPE student? Wasn't all of that enough? Wasn't I already a "fine pastor"?

THE CHALLENGE FOR THE PASTOR

Movement from a point of being an enthusiastic young pastor to being one who feels she or he is a spiritual leader in a particular church setting is quite a journey. It is challenging in many ways. The journey's ultimate end is inclusion, being aware that we are connected to God and to others. This means both having a sense of belonging and being hospitable to others. Being hospitable is a natural outcome of inclusion. We feel divine hospitality when we are aware of belonging to God. We feel this hospitality in our devotional life and we feel it in our church membership. This experience of hospitality is so good that we have to share it. Sharing it means moving beyond our natural boundaries and reaching out to others.

I served as pastor of the Buckingham Charge for four years. During those four years I became comfortable in my role as their pastor. I came to understand the people and their culture. In time I came to understand myself as a member of their community. I came to understand myself as a spiritual leader. This journey was possible through God's grace. It involved God's nurture of me. That nurture was often done through the nurture of those three churches.

THE CHALLENGE FOR THE CHURCH

The woman who predicted my coming spiritual growth put her finger on the challenge the small membership church faces. Small membership churches often have pastors who are new to ministry. Like me during my years at the Buckingham Charge, many of these pastors have some training, education, and experience. They may have lots of energy and enthusiasm for ministry.

Spiritual leadership for small membership churches is often a journey in nurture. The congregations help train and mold the pastor to a point of competence and then the pastor moves on to a bigger church. If the pastor learns quickly he or she often moves more quickly. This means that small membership churches often spend much of their time and energy training, and therefore they have limited opportunity to enjoy the fruits of their labors.

Small membership churches have other unique challenges. Intimacy takes on a whole new meaning when members of a congregation are so few that they all know each other well. Often small membership congregations are made up of only a few families. This means that separating family issues from church issues may be very complicated or even impossible. The level of intimacy that the people have with each other may make it difficult to accept outsiders. The pastor may have a difficult time becoming an accepted member of the faith community. People of differing ethnic backgrounds may have a difficult time becoming accepted as members of the faith community. Thus intimacy may be a hindrance to inclusion and hospitality.

ENDINGS

My wife, Judy, and I read books differently. I'm constantly looking at the last page to find how much I have left to read. Judy will never look at the last page. She doesn't want to risk knowing how the story will end. Her enjoyment of reading seems to be journeying through each page. My enjoyment of reading seems to be in getting to the end of the story. When you read, do you look forward to the end of the book or article? Or does your satisfaction come from the very act of reading? Many of us think about endings and pray for them. In a spiritual sense we wonder if we are headed in the right direction or if we are doing what God wants us to do with our lives.

Every year we observe Columbus Day. Recently there has been a lot of controversy about Columbus and his journey to the New World. Someone wrote in a joking way that he started a journey without really knowing where he was going, when he arrived he did not know where he was, and when he returned home he did not know where he had been.

I talked with a friend who was retiring after a very full and successful career. I had discussed some of my frustrations with him, and was surprised to discover that his journey and mine were similar in many ways. Finally I asked him the question that summed up a lot of my frustration with the way I was feeling about my life. "When," I asked him, "did you begin to realize that you were doing what God wanted you to do?" He stopped, looked at me, and suddenly laughed, "I guess that I don't know that yet."

Many of us have questions today about endings in our own lives. We may sit here wondering if the journey is taking us where it is supposed to. We may have questions about what the end will be like.

God's purposes continue to unfold in our history. We are on our own journeys, yet they are not really our journeys alone. We are all a part of a larger plan that is unfolding. Spiritual leadership is the art or process through which the leader helps others move through their spiritual journey. Through this process the pastor and the church grow closer to God and to each other. This growth often begins with the pastor. It takes place both individually and collectively. Ultimately this growth is expressed in inclusion and hospitality.

CHAPTER 1

What Is Spiritual Leadership?

Spiritual leadership is the art or practice through which the leader helps others move toward spiritual maturation. One of my early supervisors spoke of it in terms of the exodus. He would use the image of a pastor leading the people to the promised land. In this context the promised land is a state of spiritual maturity. Think of Moses as the spiritual leader who brought the Hebrews from slavery to freedom. For the small membership church this state of freedom expresses itself in terms of inclusion and hospitality. Think of Moses as the spiritual leader who brought the Hebrews to a deeper state of spiritual maturity through presenting them with God's covenant. For the small membership church this covenant is God's promise to be with them collectively and individually through their entire faith journey. To go back to the example of the exodus, it was during the journey through the wilderness that the Hebrews became a nation able to settle the promised land.

The small membership church is made up of individual believers. Each has his or her faith journey. At another level the congregation has its own faith journey. The small membership church is thus not simply a group of individuals on spiritual quests. It is also a community of faith on a spiritual pilgrimage. As the congregation moves toward maturity the individual members have a heightened awareness of their communal life and their collective relationship to God. It is the role of the pastor as spiritual leader to help the small membership church move toward this deeper stage of spiritual maturity. Spiritual maturity can give us divine vision. By that I mean that we can grow spiritually until we begin to be able to see things as God sees them. It can also give us a type of spiritual hearing so that we can better hear God speak to us. This deep spiritual maturity will ultimately express itself in hospitality and inclusion. It will also express itself in a congregation that is better able to handle the pressures and conflicts that life brings.

SPIRITUAL FORMATION

Before looking at spiritual leadership in depth it is important to consider spiritual formation. This is necessary to better understand how spiritual maturity is formed within the individual or community. It is important to consider what this maturation process is.

Sometimes I hear people speaking of spiritual formation and must confess that I am not sure what they are talking about. You may have the same problem. How does spiritual formation work in the life of the believer? How does it work in the life of the small membership church? In answering these questions it is important to know that the topic of spiritual formation appears in many different contexts in our culture today. It seems to mean many different things. Indeed, words like *spiritual formation*, *spiritual experience*, *spiritual values*, and *spirituality* have all become quite popular. There are business seminars being offered on spiritual values. Addiction recovery through the Twelve Steps is a spiritual program, and it defines sobriety as a spiritual awakening. Politicians sometimes talk about spirituality or spiritual values. Celebrities appear on talk shows discussing spiritual experiences. To those of us who are called to be spiritual leaders in the church, this may all seem a bit confusing.

STAGES OF SPIRITUAL GROWTH

The stages of spiritual growth apply to the pastor, the individual members of the congregation, and to the congregation as a body. They are often difficult to observe and measure. They do not necessarily happen in any particular order. They may not happen according to a particular time schedule. Keep in mind that spiritual formation is largely a mysterious matter. We observe parts of it. We may say that we observe shadows of it. As Psalm 77:19 observes, even during mighty acts God's footprints may be unseen. We do know that all spiritual growth takes place within the context of grace—God's unconditional love.

Instincts

The first stage of spiritual growth is instincts or feelings. Instinct means an attitude or natural inclination toward something. Within me and, I believe, within others as well, there is a primal instinct for survival and fulfillment. Within all of us there is a yearning to find love, acceptance, peace, and joy. We are searching for what will give meaning to our lives. A famous theologian was struggling with this when he wrote about the soul being restless until it rests with God. This basic, instinctive part of our being can be an important way in which we experience God.

There are many ways in which God speaks to our instincts or feelings. Reading through the Psalms, for example, can be a wonderful experience in letting God help you become aware of many of your feelings. The Psalms express the whole range of human emotions. Grief, fear, joy, sadness, anger, love, thanksgiving, mistrust, worry, frustration, weariness, comfort, and hope are all found within the Psalms. Many people have trouble expressing their feelings to God in prayer. Reading the Psalms gives us all good examples of how to turn over all of our feelings to God.

God also speaks to us through our feelings as we encounter the world around us. The Bible begins with the story of creation. It is such a powerful theme that it is told twice—in both Genesis 1 and 2. In so doing, our Scriptures tell us and then repeat to us the fact that the world is a creation of God and that it is good. Consider your feelings about nature. Sunsets, sunrises, the wind blowing through the trees on an autumn day, the cold wind on a February night all stir feelings within me. Opening your senses to the world around you and seeing, smelling, touching, tasting, and hearing the creation can awaken feelings within you that can put you in touch with God.

God often communicates with us at a feeling level through others. If you are a parent, remember the first time you held your child. What did it feel like? What does it feel like to remember this experience now? Our children, our parents, our marriage partners, and our friends all arouse feelings of warmth, joy, and comfort. They may also bring feelings of discomfort and sadness. Those closest to us usually arouse the most intense feelings. Think of the ways that God speaks to you through your feelings toward others. Even the people we see through the media cause certain feelings within us. The events of September 11, 2001, have made many previously unknown faces familiar to us. Many of them we now consider enemies. How do we feel about our enemies? Most of us experience conflict when we think of enemies. We may experience a mixture of anger and guilt. Some of the guilt may come from remembering that Jesus spoke of having love for our enemies. Let your feelings toward your enemies be a channel through which God speaks to your spirit.

Years ago a spiritual director taught me that our feelings play an important part in not only hearing God, but also in finding direction from God. It is simple, but we sometimes miss it. If we feel pretty good about a decision, that is one sign that it is the desire of God. If we feel uncomfortable or guilty about a decision, that is one sign that it may be in conflict with the will of God.

Feelings are important. God does indeed speak to you through your feelings. In order to better hear and understand the word of God as it comes through your feelings, listen to your faith, listen to the world around you, and listen to others.

Insights

The next spiritual stage we move into is insight or knowing. It has to do with learning and making connections. During the late-1960s I was in seminary and can remember being frustrated because I could not *find* God through my academic studies. This is not to say that seminary frustrated me. Actually, I enjoyed seminary and found it to be a most positive experience. However, systematic theology, philosophy of religion, and church history did not seem helpful in my search for a loving God. I mentioned this to my theology professor and he laughed and said, "You aren't supposed to find God in theology." I asked him why I was reading theology, then, and he replied, "To graduate from seminary. You don't find God in theology though. You find God in the Bible and in the lives of the saints." His words were meant to tease me and they certainly did that. They also turned me toward reading some of the spiritual classics. School exposed me to the writings of Augustine, John Wesley, and many other saints of the church. On my own I began to read about these people and to read their letters and books. Along the way I began to discover other people like Teresa of Avila, Julian of Norwich, Thomas à Kempis, Brother Lawrence, Thomas Kelly, and many others. However, I became interested in them not just as figures in church history, but more important as great souls who helped me experience the presence of God in powerful ways in my everyday life. Their writings became powerful parts of my devotional life. These souls began to feel like mentors and friends to me. When I took my new friends back to the study of theology they began to help me understand theology at profound new levels. It was not that I was finding God there, but rather that through reflecting on their works I moved to new levels of spiritual maturity that helped me to understand not only God, but also the church and even my own life in deeper ways. I liked that.

Because of my study of the saints, I began to understand the people in my churches as living saints. I also began to reflect back on the Sunday school teachers and Methodist Youth Fellowship counselors from my youth. Through my relationships with these people my awareness of God deepened. New appreciation began to develop within me of the dynamic relationship that exists between pastors and parishioners and the church itself through which all may grow in their understanding of God and all have the opportunity to grow closer to God.

You probably do not know the people who have influenced me spiritually—the people who have helped me mature and come closer to God. I wish you had known Miss Lucy Elliott. She was a friend of my grandparents and knew my parents since their birth. For some reason she insisted on calling me "the little preacher" when I was just a child. I do not know what she saw in me, but her words and her Sunday school classes helped bring me closer to God. I wish you had known Lorene Clowdis. She was my seventh grade teacher, my elementary school principal, and in the latter years of her life she was my dear friend. She was demanding as a teacher. She always expected a lot of all her students. She somehow instilled in me a curiosity and joy about God and all of creation. When I was a young pastor we would see each other every year at annual conference. She would always go out to dinner with my wife and me. We had great times talking about life and about our journeys. Leo and Harriett Garrett still walk the earth and I remember them as teachers and subdistrict youth leaders. They remain close friends. These are just a few of the people who are saints in my life. There are so many others that I wish I had the opportunity to tell you about each of them. If you think about it you will surely come up with your own list of saints—people who have helped you mature spiritually. People who helped you experience the presence of God.

Some of our insights are just facts we know. Knowing the truth is very important to the Gospel of John. For John, knowing the truth means knowing who Jesus is—the Son of God the Savior of the world. In John 8:32 we have a good example of how something we know can change us. Jesus said, "And you will know the truth, and the truth will make you free." Another verse to consider is Psalm 19:14. It addresses our thoughts by saying: "Let the words of my mouth and the meditation of my heart be acceptable to you, O LORD, my rock and my redeemer." Preachers often use this verse as a prayer before giving a sermon. The words focus our thoughts on pleasing God. They remind us of the importance of pleasing God in our lives and ask God to direct our thoughts. What if every church member would pray this prayer before speaking in a church meeting?

Our thoughts may sort data, state what we know to be true, and apply that knowledge to the world around us. However, insight has another component. Our thoughts have the ability to become imaginative and can help us envision things that do not exist at this point. Imagination has to do with thinking about possibilities for your life. Imagination also has to do with thinking about possibilities for your congregation. The three members who worship at a tiny church may see themselves growing older. Getting to and from church on Sunday may become a burden. They may see the neighborhood around the church begin to change. African American and Mexican families begin to move in. As they observe themselves and the surrounding community they begin to imagine ways that God is calling them to be the church in their community in a new way.

The Bible is filled with many flights of imagination that take us to a world that does not as yet exist here. The Revelation to John is certainly one of the most imaginative of books in the Bible. The vision of the new heaven and earth, the vision of the new Jerusalem in chapter 21, is certainly one of the most beautiful things in the entire Bible. It was first read by Christians at a time when the church was going through great persecution that threatened the lives of believers and even seemed to threaten the life of the church itself. Through reading and thinking about this vision they found strength and hope that helped them endure. As *we* think about it and meditate on it, it changes us. It begins to give us a kind of strength and hope that it gave Christians almost two thousand years ago. Our hardship is different. The members of the tiny church are concerned about how to keep worshiping together when health and the process of aging make it difficult for them to get to church. They may sacrifice to keep paying the bills at the church and may wonder how they can, on fixed incomes, continue to pay the electric bill. The presence of a loving God remains the same for the members at the tiny church as it was for the first century church in Asia Minor. God wipes away our tears. In our thoughts God becomes real and our tears begin to dry.

God calls each of us. By focusing our thoughts on God we can better hear God through our thoughts. As we focus our thoughts on God we then learn. Learning offers endless possibilities for activities and programs in the church. As God shapes our thoughts God teaches us what we are to know in order to better serve as disciples of Jesus.

Initiative

Initiative or doing begins to move us beyond feeling and thinking. The things we do often provide the easiest ways to hear God's call and feel God's presence in our lives. Most of us stay so busy that it is difficult to remember much of what we do. Our lives stay so packed with activities that remembering what we do on a particular day is difficult. Learning to hear God's call through our actions first requires that we begin to *understand* our own actions. All of us wonder at times why we do some of the things we do. Coming to a better understanding of our actions involves examining our routines, values, and interests.

All of our lives are built around particular routines. This is true of us individually and as a congregation. When I arrive at a new pastoral appointment I make learning the routine of the congregations my highest priority. I don't change anything until I find out how and why things operate the way they do. If the church holds an annual barbeque on the second Saturday of November, it follows that carrying out this event will shape some of the church activities. If worship and Sunday school take place at a particular time, the timing of those events shapes the activities of the congregation. Prayer meetings, committee meetings, Bible study groups, and support groups are activities that shape the life of the congregation. These activities are possible for us because we plan them into our busy schedules. We make them a priority. For most Christians the entire weekly schedule centers around attendance at worship. I often hear people say "The week just doesn't feel right if I don't begin it by going to church."

Think about the kinds of things that fill the church calendar. It may teach you something about the congregation's priorities and values. Have your administrative council and various committees prioritize the things they do. Remind them that where they put their time and energy reflects their values. Have them talk about those values and decide whether they need to rethink the things they do. Pastors often feel they have little or no control over the church calendar. If you truly feel squeezed and think you have no control over your schedule it would be a good idea to pray with the calendar in front of you and ask God to help you understand how choice plays a part in setting your routine. It is always a good thing to prayerfully consider how you spend your time.

Perhaps this inventory of the church schedule will reveal some activities that do damage to us or those we love. All of us have heard the old saying, "Your actions speak so loudly that I can't hear your words." Someone has said that our lives will be the only Bible that many people ever read. If you or I live with constant feelings of guilt perhaps it means that we have done or are doing things that are harmful. Consider how the activities of your congregation impact the lives of others. Ask God to lead you and the congregation away from damaging or destructive activities and into positive activities. Perhaps God is trying to speak with you and with your congregation through some of the painful things you are involved in today.

One of the spiritual disciplines is deeds of kindness and mercy. Hearing God's call is easier when we are doing things for others. The church offers countless ways to do acts of kindness. As pastor, make a special effort to advertise, talk about, and encourage church members to be involved in such acts within the church program and within the community. Hearing God's call is easier when we are doing things for others. Offering to take a neighbor to church is an act of kindness. Offering to take someone to a medical appointment is an act of kindness. Many church members volunteer for Habitat for Humanity, a local hospital, a nursing home, or a shelter. Several years ago it came to my attention that our local pastors' association was sending only male pastors to conduct worship at the local shelter for battered women. I mentioned this to several women at one of my churches and a couple of them volunteered to start taking Holy Communion to the shelter. Participation increased dramatically. They also began a monthly evening prayer service. Take the time to encourage church members in these types of endeavors. Remind them to thank God for the opportunity they have to serve. Ask them to ask God to let them hear the divine voice calling through their actions.

Our actions have a lot to do with shaping us individually and as a congregation. Many actions involve receiving and many actions involve giving. Too often we consider an activity worthwhile if we get something good out of it. Churches are not immune to this. We may value the new family in the community for what they can contribute to the life of the congregation. I constantly remind myself and our people that in Acts 20:35 we are reminded that Jesus taught us that it is more blessed to give than to receive. Do our actions mark us as *givers* or *takers*? The prayer of Saint Francis of Assisi has helped Christians hear God's call for centuries. It does so through focusing us on the actions that follow our calling as God's children. Try having your congregation pray it from time to time: "Lord, make me an instrument of thy peace. / Where there is hatred, let me sow love; / where there is injury, pardon; / where there is doubt, faith; / where there is despair, hope; / where there is darkness, light; / and where there is sadness, joy. / O Divine Master, / grant that I may not so much seek / to be consoled as to console; / to be understood, as to understand; / to be loved as to love; / for it is in giving that we receive; / it is in pardoning that we are pardoned; / and it is in dying that we are born to eternal life" (*The United Methodist Hymnal* [Nashville: United Methodist Publishing House, 1989], 481).

Integrity

A deeper stage of spiritual formation is that of integrity or being. Integrity is the point of congruence where our feelings, thoughts, and actions are not in conflict. It is a point at which our feelings, thoughts, and actions all flow from what we are at the core of our being. What we believe, what we think, and what we do have become so integrated that we are what we are. This means that if you see me at church, at the supermarket, in your home, or at school that I will be the same person. I do not have a different set of actions, or beliefs, or feelings for these different parts of my life. Before God, before my family, before my friends, when alone, I am always the same person.

All of us would like to live this way. It would mean that we are at peace with ourselves, others, and God. It would mean that we have no feelings of guilt because we profess one thing and live another. Getting there requires discipline, patience, and practice. Integrity is an end product of a growth process that often requires eternity. In other words, it is begun in this life but only gets completely worked out in heaven. In Hebrews 6:1 the writer says that we must go on toward perfection. John Wesley treasured that verse, and to this day all United Methodist clergy must take a vow when they are ordained to go on toward perfection. The word *perfection* actually comes from a Greek word meaning *maturity*. Think of your own life. Think of the life of the congregation. Think of what the word *integrity* means for both.

If you play a musical instrument you will understand how integrity works. Playing a scale requires that you think of the mechanics of it—how the hands, fingers, lips, or your breathing work on your instrument. You must also listen to how the notes sound and think of the tonal progression they need to make. After a while you have so trained your body in the practice of the scale that it is done without conscious thought. The same thing works spiritually. You do something enough times and it becomes a part of you. It also works with a congregation. When the Apostles' Creed is read weekly, it can soon be recited. Over time it becomes internalized, and then it is lived as a part of faith and a part of life for the gathered community.

The same is true of the things you say in your sermons. There are certain teachings in the Bible that I believe are central to our lives as Christians. One of these is God's steadfast love. I base my weekly sermons on the lectionary, which covers many themes, but a large percentage of them include, somewhere in the sermon, the phrase, "God loves you so much. . . ." I realized that this constant repetition was accomplishing its purpose when an elderly gentleman whose theology had always been centered on anger and God's judgment said during a Sunday school class discussion, "It's just that God loves us so much. . . ." He was getting the message. It was becoming a part of his vocabulary and his thoughts. He was beginning to experience a God of love.

Patience cannot be overstated as an important trait to bring to the process of integration. John Wesley loved Philippians 2:12-13: "Work out your own salvation with fear and trembling; for it is God who is at work in you, enabling you both to will and to work for his good pleasure." Salvation is seen here as a process or a journey toward holiness. It takes time and work. Remember that this process would not be possible were it not for the God who is at work in you and in the congregation. Ultimately it is not your work, or my work, or their work. It is God's work. Our disciplines, our work, our life together are simply a conscious turning of our lives toward God. It is practicing what we think, how we feel, and how we act so that over time it comes more in line with what is acceptable and pleasing to God. Too often we become impatient with ourselves and with our congregation and we forget that God is very patient. God is love. God is eternal. What seems to take us a lifetime to incorporate into our lives takes no time at all in the eternity of God. Paul reminds us that this working of God within us is a matter of *divine good pleasure*. In other words, God enjoys seeing us work at it.

All churches are becoming. As spiritual leaders we must always remember that. All churches are in the process of integrating what they feel, what they know, and what they do. To have not reached a state of perfection or maturity is not necessarily a bad thing. We and our churches are becoming, and God is taking pleasure in our struggles, our successes, and our journey.

As we become a people of integrity we find that our thoughts, feelings, and actions become more congruent. The inner conflicts that have caused us so much pain grow fewer in number. We become happier with ourselves and with our neighbors. We become more content with the circumstances of our lives. The less conflicted we are the more we are able to hear and respond to the call of God. The less conflicted we are the more we grow into a healthy, fruit bearing garden.

To say something we must first *be* something. Let the spiritual disciplines and practices of the daily and weekly life of the church mold us so that we may *be* the people of integrity that God envisioned us at our creation. Know that God patiently enjoys seeing us work out our salvation in the daily and weekly experiences of congregational life.

Inclusion

The above model of spiritual formation with four stages of spiritual growth made sense to me for about ten years. It seemed to me that instincts, insights, initiative, and integrity outlined our growing from spiritual infancy to maturity. Some months ago, however, I began to understand that there is a deeper stage of spiritual growth. This stage can be called *inclusion*. It is a stage of *reaching out* toward others. It is a stage in which boundaries begin to fall away. It is a stage in which God calls us to move beyond ourselves and open ourselves not only to the divine call, but also to the call of others in the world around us. It is this stage to which Jesus calls us through the Great Commission of Matthew 28:19-20.

Some time ago I heard of a pastor who challenged the people of his congregation to begin to pray that God would send them the people that no other church wanted. Since that time I have challenged my people to pray the same thing. To whom is our welcome extended? One well-known pastor told me that his church had found its life by extending hospitality to the homeless of their community. In so doing, he told me, they have learned that life is found through giving to those who are powerless to return their gifts. This is, of course, scriptural. Two of our churches are currently doing a Bible study of the Gospel According to Luke. Whenever I read any part of Luke I am struck by how inclusive Jesus' message is. Tax collectors, Roman soldiers, Gentiles, women, a Samaritan, a prostitute, a Gentile possessed by demons, children, the sick, and the hungry all have a special place in Jesus' heart in Luke. The list could go on. In this wonderful Gospel the touch of Jesus goes out to all who are marginalized. In Luke 14:12-14 Jesus tells us to invite to our banquet those who cannot repay the favor. Jesus' compassion is not limited to Luke's Gospel, however. Matthew 25:31-46 is the parable of the Sheep and the Goats. It is a parable of the Last Judgment. Jesus tells his followers that when they have looked at the marginalized they have seen him, and that if they have failed to take care of those unloved by society, they have failed to take care of Jesus. Jesus' radical identification with the least of our world calls us to move beyond our own doors and to extend hospitality to all who are in need.

Another of the most powerful scriptural witnesses to inclusion is found in 1 John 4:7-21. It is a remarkable testimony to the power of love and to God's call to love. It ends with a challenge to the church: "Those who say 'I love God,' and hate their brothers or sisters, are liars; for those who do not love a brother or sister whom they have seen, cannot love God whom they have not seen. The commandment we have from him is this: those who love God must love their brothers and sisters also" (vv. 20-21). The love of God always calls on us to move beyond our walls and love others for whom Christ died.

Use your sermons to emphasize the fact that God loves all people. What are the attitudes of your church members toward people of other races and cultures? Do they understand the conflict caused by saying that they love God but don't love people who are different from themselves? Do they include in their fellowship people who have different sexual preferences from their own or do these people who are a part of every community have to keep their sexuality hidden in order to be accepted? How does your congregation feel about those who are, or are perceived as, the enemy? Jesus said that we should love our enemies. Do you include our enemies in your pastoral prayer on Sunday morning? Talk with your administrative council about what it means to exclude people. Talk about what it means to be inclusive.

A young couple has a child with severe birth defects. When the young mother brought the child to church the pastor and congregation seemed annoyed with the baby's crying and offered no special services. A nearby church began taking love offerings to help with the child's medical expenses. The women's group and Sunday school classes sent cards to the family. Within a year the family moved its membership to the church that showed love and hospitality toward them and their baby.

Two decades ago a small rural white church's administrative council voted not to allow African Americans to worship there. Ten years later a different pastor invited an African American church youth choir to sing at a revival. This opened the doors to other opportunities to worship together.

These are simple acts, but they speak of a congregation's progress toward inclusion. Inclusion also means taking care of the practical issues that tend to exclude people and make them feel less than welcome. The church must remove all obstacles that make it hard for people to attend and participate. One of our congregations is now working on plans to install an elevator in our building. We are also working on plans to have our worship service broadcast into the lower level of the church for our members who are not able to climb stairs. A congregation must always ask if the building itself and then its programs are designed to make people with special needs feel wanted. Consider fellowship dinners. Are menu items provided for people with special dietary needs?

SPIRITUAL LEADERSHIP AS SHARED RESPONSIBILITY

It is important to know that as the pastor leads the pastor is also led. As the pastor shapes the pastor is also shaped. The art of spiritual leadership does not take place in a vacuum. It is in the day in and day out give-and-take of ministry that both the pastor and the small membership church are spiritually formed or moved toward maturity.

The pastor, as spiritual leader, must be able to articulate a vision. Through preaching, pastoral care, teaching, administration of the sacraments, and administration of the church program the pastor expresses his or her vision. However, that vision is a product of the pastor's own spiritual awareness and the awareness and needs of the people.

As the pastor is forming as a spiritual leader, the small membership church is also forming as a spiritual community. This formation takes place individually and collectively. As the small membership church grows spiritually it becomes more able to express its needs. Individually and collectively the members develop a deeper understanding of themselves as connected to God and each other. They want to share their awareness of belonging to God. They begin to understand God's claim on all people, and God's love for all people.

CHAPTER 2

The Pastor as Spiritually Forming Leader

THE SETTING

I sit here in my parsonage office and listen to the ticking of the clock. It is morning. I am in contemplative prayer. I hear the birds outside the window. I also hear a car several streets over. This small town—Burkeville, Virginia—is home to only five hundred thirty-five people. When I call my friend Hyun Mi in Manhattan I can always hear cars passing and honking outside her apartment window. This quiet place is quite different from her home. For a moment I consider Burkeville and Manhattan. Not all places are alike. The sights and sounds of different places touch different parts of my soul. Burkeville is my particular place at this point in my life. It is the space in which I live, move, and have my being. My three churches are all different. Each has its own sights and sounds.

Again I listen to the sound of the ticking of the clock. Time is the same all over the world. A minute in Burkeville is the same as a minute in Manhattan. I think of this particular moment as I hear its passage sounded by the ticking. I realize that it is a gift from God. It is in this time that I live, move, and have my being. Again, I think of my three churches. I have been their pastor for three years. Three years here are quantitatively the same as three years in any other place. The three years are a gift God has given to me and to the churches.

The ticking also reminds me that there is no time in eternity. God somehow dwells beyond time. There is no space in eternity. God, too, somehow dwells beyond space. At another level I am aware that God is also here with me in this parsonage office. Somehow God is wonderfully in this small town of five hundred thirty-five people. God is wonderfully in my three churches. God is also with me at this particular time. I sit among the spirits of centuries of pastors who have gone before me. I think of the cemeteries outside my churches. The cemeteries are the resting places of our past leaders. Somehow the past leaders of these three churches are also here with me. They, too, are beyond this time and space, and yet they are very much present here. A desire to grow closer to God and to those former pastors and parishioners—those saints—drives me. Now I realize that somehow I have moved beyond this time and space and that my spirit transcends the bounds of my physical journey. Somehow a part of me is in eternity. I am united with God and with those who have gone before me in a mysterious and wonderfully blessed way.

The three churches of the Burkeville United Methodist Charge have been joined together in one pastoral appointment for one hundred one years. Ward's Chapel is the largest church with 164 members. Bethel is next in size with 72 members. Salem has 28 members—only three of them remain active. The three churches are in three adjoining counties. Each Sunday morning I make a circuit of 31 miles to conduct worship in each church. Each of these worship services begins with a responsive reading of one of the Psalms. These three churches are all so very different. Each has its own personality. Each has its own spirit. Each reads the Psalms differently. Yet each calls on God at the appointed hour. I remember that God somehow dwells beyond time. Each church assembles at the same place they and their ancestors have worshiped for over a century. There is no space in eternity. God dwells beyond time and space. At another level the members of those three churches and I are aware that God is also with us in those three churches and at those hours. When we gather to worship we sit among the spirits of centuries of believers who have gone before us. A desire to have us grow closer to each other and to God and to those former believers drives us. Maybe all of the members do not realize what is happening, but they, too, are moving beyond time and space in their worship. They are in some mysterious and wonderful way entering eternity. As pastor of the churches I desire to help lead others to a deeper awareness and a deeper experience of this divine presence and this divine reality. This drawing closer to God is done through a process of spiritual formation.

THE PROCESS

A few weeks ago I talked about life with my doctor. She is a dedicated church member. She laughed and said that sometimes she thinks the church adds to our stress level by continually teaching us that we are on a journey. There may be some truth to what she says. Too often I find myself believing that I am constantly reaching for something beyond my grasp. I always seem to be adjusting to new situations in my life and work. Although these new situations are a big part of this spiritual journey, they bring stress. Perhaps the greatest gift of understanding my journey in a spiritual context is that it helps me move beyond the stress. It actually enables me to transcend my particular time and space and be united with God and the saints in eternity. In so doing it lifts me far enough away from the stresses of my time and space that I am able to look down on them from a different perspective—a divine perspective.

All spiritual leadership is a gift of the Holy Spirit. It is of God and reflects God's ongoing presence in our lives at every moment. As stated above, the very fact that we are able to experience God at all is a gift of God. God's Holy Spirit dwells within each of us and that spirit leads us into understanding. The spirit teaches us about God and the spirit teaches us about ourselves. It not only teaches, but it leads and guides and molds us. That which drives me to a deeper understanding of God and a deeper relationship with God is the Holy Spirit at work within me.

THE PARABLE—A GARDEN

Spiritual leadership in the small membership church, I believe, usually starts from the devotional life of the pastor. Consider the pastor's own spiritual formation. Think of the example of a garden. Part of my fascination with gardens comes from the creation story in Genesis. It tells us that we humans were created for life in a garden. Indeed, one of Jesus' most remarkable parables is about a garden. Another part of my fascination with gardens comes from my wife's gardening.

Wherever we live my wife, Judy, starts a garden. She grew up on a farm and has been around plants and gardens all her life. That background does not make gardening easy for her, however. The process of preparing the soil for her plants goes on year after year, and is always hard work. Every year she not only tills the soil but she continues to prepare the soil for her seed or plants. This process involves mixing peat moss, compost, or manure into the soil. Because of my different assignments we have moved every few years. This makes her task more difficult. We lived in Maryland for six years, and during our last year there she felt the soil was in pretty good shape. We lived in Korea for four years, and during our last year there she thought the soil was acceptable. We lived in El Paso, Texas, for three years, and that desert sand needed a lot more care and nurture than even her experienced hands could give it in that short period of time.

One of the most remarkable parables Jesus told was that of the sower (Matt 13:1-9). This parable is unique in that it is the only parable that Jesus explains or interprets (13:18-23). Normally a parable is like a good joke or a good story. It speaks for itself. The more that is said to explain it the more the meaning may become clouded. Some scholars have thought that the explanation to this parable may have been the interpretation used by the church and may have been a later editorial addition to the parable. That may be, but it may also be true that Jesus felt this parable was so important that it needed an explanation so that its meaning would not be missed by his followers. The interpretation explains the parable as allegory. It indicates that the sower and every object in the parable represent something beyond themselves. It tells us that God, the sower, plants the divine word in all kinds of places. The word of God is many things. It is the good news that Jesus Christ is God in the flesh and that through him we are given eternal life. The Word is God's love. The Word is the very presence of God. The places are, of course, the hearts or spirits of different people. The places where the seed is sown may also be small membership churches. Some people and communities of faith hear with joy but they have no deep soil—spiritual awareness—in which the word of God can take root. Other people and churches may have a capacity for deep spiritual truth but the cares and pressures of this life make it impossible for God's word to grow within them. Other people and small membership churches have spiritual lives that Jesus refers to as "good soil." These are the people and faith communities who hear God's word, understand it, and then have it grow within them. As God's word grows within them it leads through a maturation process that brings the believers to a point of spiritual growth. This growth results in fruits of God's spirit being manifest in the believer's life. Paul says that these fruits are "love, joy, peace, patience, kindness, generosity, faithfulness, gentleness, and self-control" (Gal 5:22-23).

All of us want these spiritual fruits in our lives. All of us want to see our churches demonstrate an outpouring of love that is available to all people and that beckons all people into the presence of God. Most of us experience the pain of not being what we want to be or what we believe God wants us to be. Most of us are aware that our churches fall far short of being the gracious communities of faith for which Christ gave his life. How are we to become people and churches that are good soil for God's word? How are we to become pastors who help other people and help our churches become good soil for God's word? Much time and energy in today's world seems to be spent telling us how to be prosperous or successful. Having lives that bear the spiritual gifts mentioned above does not necessarily lead to success or power or financial wealth. In fact, our spiritual lives may take us to places that seem far from things that the world's values may readily identify as "good." The most spiritually mature small membership church may remain small and may be impoverished in the eyes of the world. Even our denomination may tempt us into believing that numerical growth in our churches should be the highest good we can strive for, and that professional growth in ministry involves promotion to a bigger church. Our spiritual growth may lead us into a very different awareness.

THE SPIRITUAL LIFE OF THE PASTOR— PREPARING THE SOWER

How are we to become pastors who are aware of the good news of God's love in deep ways? How are we to become pastors who are aware of the presence of God in all the events of our lives? How are we to become pastors who can lead our small membership churches to a point of spiritual maturity? Many of the great spirits of our faith have written about the *divine awareness* as something we all have within us. This awareness is the grace that helps us begin to get to know God. We pastors must face the challenge of knowing how to grow in our awareness of the presence of God before we can begin to lead others in an intentional way. Using the images found in the parable of the Sower, we begin by focusing on ways we can become good soil in which the word of God will grow and bear fruit.

Having a greater awareness of God's presence requires that we first prepare the soil of our hearts and spirits as my wife prepares the soil of her garden. God is already preparing our spirits for the experience of divine presence. It begins with God's action in our world. It begins with the action of God in our churches. It begins with the action of God specifically in our lives. God also provides ways for us to respond to this grace that is already operative.

Consider the image of the garden in Jesus' parable. As God is the sower who casts seed of love, so you, too, are called to be a sower who casts the seed of God's word. As you are sowing the seed in the lives of your people and your churches, God is sowing seed in your life.

Consider your own spiritual life. How do we prepare the soil—our hearts and spirits—to be better able to produce fruits of the spirit? There are a number of spiritual disciplines that have been used since the earliest days of the church to help us on the journey toward spiritual maturity. We all use some of them, but few of us use them to the degree that is most beneficial. These disciplines are often called *means of grace*.

These practices include: Bible study, prayer, attendance at public worship, acts of kindness and mercy, spiritual friendship or direction, and receiving Holy Communion. Do you set aside parts of each day for the intentional practice of these disciplines? Each day should begin in prayer, Bible study, and reflection. For the pastor this may be more difficult than it seems. Small membership church pastors tend to have to work a lot of evenings. When I get home after an evening meeting I usually need time to relax and unwind emotionally before going to bed. This often means that I am late getting to bed. All too often the phone rings early in the morning and calls me into some unexpected pastoral care situation or emergency. It is often very difficult to find times and places where I can worship as a member of the congregation or receive Holy Communion. Actually, deeds of kindness and mercy are often the only spiritual discipline that is routine for most clergy.

Recently a fine pastor told me about a difficult time she had conducting an important committee meeting. She told me that part of the problem was that she had driven the thirty miles to the meeting with another pastor. While she enjoyed the company of the other minister, she reflected that when she travels alone she uses the time on the road to spiritually center herself with prayer. I do the same thing. Long trips to the hospital or to meetings can be wonderful times for prayer and reflection—for consciously seeking the presence of God. Pastors are normally surrounded by others, and that time of quiet and solitude is most important for us.

My mornings always begin with a period of prayer and meditation, Bible reading, and other devotional reading. Mine is obviously not the only approach to prayer and study, but I will share what works for me. Immediately after showering in the morning I make coffee and get a bowl of oatmeal. I take them to my study and sit down to read the Bible. For about four years I have been reading five psalms a day. In this way I work my way through the entire Psalter every month. Over time I have developed a pattern that varies a bit from month to month. Normally when I reach Psalm 119 I use that for my Psalter reading for the day. The following day I read Psalms 120 to 134, the Psalms of Ascents. Once in a while I will spend a month with a commentary and study one or two of the psalms each day. Normally I use the New Revised Standard Version of the Bible, but occasionally I will spend the month reading the Psalter in a different translation. After reading the Psalter I normally do a devotion that is based on the weekly lectionary lesson.

For many years I faithfully used the Revised Common Lectionary in worship preparation without fully appreciating its use as a guide to personal daily devotions. If you are from the Free Church tradition you may not be familiar with the lectionary. The lectionary is more than suggested readings for Sunday. It is a guide for the celebration of the church year. The church year is based on the life, death, resurrection, and ascension of Jesus. Beginning four weeks before Christmas, at Advent, and continuing through a twelve-month cycle it celebrates all the major events of the life of Christ. It celebrates all of the holidays and seasons of the church year. By using the lectionary in my personal devotions I am intentionally placing my spiritual life within the context of Christ's life and ministry and within the context of the church's worship services. My spiritual life is thus shaped by the rhythms of the life of the church.

One pastor told me that he never uses lectionary lessons during a time of private devotions. He told me that he did not want his personal prayer life to get mixed up with his professional role of preaching and teaching. His approach to both prayer and work seem dangerous to me. If I am going to be a pastor or preacher of integrity then it seems to me that my personal life and my professional ministry must be led and shaped by my prayer life.

Prayer cannot be emphasized enough. There are many kinds of prayer. Some have suggested that at least half of our prayer time should be spent in praise. Take the time to thank God for your life and for all the blessings you receive from God each moment. Prayers of petition are also important. I spend time on three separate days each week praying for the three churches I serve. On Mondays I pray for Ward's Chapel. On Tuesdays I pray for Bethel. On Wednesdays I pray for Salem. In that time of prayer I do not remember individual members of the churches, but rather, I pray for the community—the body. Then I do petitions for individuals. This begins with family, moves to friends, church members, the world. Then I pray for my own spiritual needs for that particular day, and I dedicate the day to God, asking God to help the day be a time of feeling the divine presence.

Several pastors I know take monthly retreats. This is one way to be able to worship and receive Holy Communion. Electronic events are not really of much help in this area. Catching a worship service on radio and television is not the same as actually sitting within the body of Christ. Look for ways to attend worship as often as possible. If you are in a clergy group, take seriously the opportunities it presents for worship and Holy Communion. If your group does not make such opportunities available you might suggest that they start.

Spiritual friendship or direction is also extremely important. During much of my ministry I have sought out someone I trusted to provide help in this area. Many denominations provide such services. Our district, for example, has chaplains who are available to help in this area. Find a trusted friend or friends to share your journey.

One layman once described his pastor to me as being "spiritually bankrupt." One of the saints of my life is Philip DeMuth. He was my pastor and friend. He used to say, "The only thing worse than an ignorant pastor is two ignorant pastors." God desires that you be neither a spiritually bankrupt nor ignorant pastor. The practice of these disciplines has led pastors in preparing the soil of their hearts and spirits since the earliest days of our faith. Consider your practices and ways that you can deepen them.

Desire is most important. Do you and I want a deeper awareness of God's presence in our lives? When someone comes to me with a personal problem I always ask the person if they are aware of where God is in their situation. It has been my experience that few of us are able to identify God's presence in the midst of our problems. Sometimes people say, "Well, I know that God loves me." That is a wonderful and insightful observation and affirmation. It is a starting place.

EXPERIENCING GOD'S PRESENCE IN TIME AND SPACE

A great philosopher wrote that we experience reality in time and space. This is pretty simple but very profound. It means that we only know things that we experience in a particular place at a particular time. This insight has many implications for the Christian life. It has many implications for the life of the pastor. One of the things it means is that what happens in the here and now is of great importance. In order to more fully understand the presence of God in our lives we must begin where we are now. This moment that you spend reading these words is important. It is more than important. It is critical. Growing in your awareness of God does not have to wait until next Sunday when you go to church. It does not have to wait until next summer when you go to the beach or the mountains and find God in a natural setting far from the pressures of daily work and routine. It does not have to wait until you go on a retreat with a clergy group this fall. It does not have to wait until you are assigned to a larger church. This is a moment when God is deeply involved in your life, and it can be the moment when you begin to grow toward a great awareness of God's presence.

This may mean that you have to let go of excuses or negative thoughts. Thoughts about not being ready, or not knowing enough, or not being good enough need to be put aside. Thoughts of waiting until you are assigned to a larger church need to be put aside. The truth is that God's presence in your life is not dependent on any of those things. Our knowledge or readiness or goodness has nothing to do with the presence of God in our lives or with our ability to respond to that presence. The truth is that none of us knows enough or is really prepared or is truly good enough to better experience God. Accepting ourselves as we are and where we are in this very moment is all that matters when we look for a starting point.

Judy's garden grows some plants even before she fully prepares the soil. In fact, she always finds that the soil is never fully prepared. She begins at the proper time—now. There is always something that can be done to plan, to enrich the soil, to plant, to weed, to mulch, to look forward to the fruits of her labor.

PASTORING AS THE DESIRE TO BLESS

All of us have unique journeys as Christians and as pastors. In my case, I was born in a rural community. In fact, my home is less than an hour's drive from the parsonage office where I am writing to you. My home church had only about twenty active members while I was growing up there. After seminary I asked for an appointment in my home district. A part of what motivated me to come home was a desire to learn to bless the area and the people who live here. I knew that I had to do this to be a more effective pastor. The great Southern Baptist pastor, Carlyle Marney, had told me that unless I could bless my own life experience— "bless where you have come from" in his words—it would be difficult for me to be a blessing to anyone else. My first appointment was with three small rural churches. During that time, however, I began to feel called to be a minister in some capacity other than the local church. This feeling led me to a point of feeling frustration with my particular time and space. I began looking to the future—a different time—and another type of ministry—a different space—as a promise of a more blessed life. This led to dissatisfaction with my given time and space. Many small membership church pastors do this. It is easy for us to see ourselves as "paying our dues" and preparing for something "better." Ministry took me to those places I was dreaming about. I became a hospital chaplain, a nursing home administrator for my denomination, and finally an army chaplain for twenty-four years. After all of that I retired from the army and returned to this small rural parish where I am in my fourth year of service. Through it all I have learned that the sacred is encountered in the *here and now*. This moment is always a time when the soil is ready—though not perfectly so. Blessing or awareness of the presence is not limited to a time and place in which we will *arrive* at a distant promised land. What matters is where you are right now.

Today, then, is the proper time and this is the proper place. Do you desire a deeper awareness of God in your life? Do you desire to more clearly feel loved by God? Do you desire to feel led by God through all the difficult places this life presents? Do you desire to be an effective pastor of your current church or churches? Do you desire to bless? The key starting point is within our own desire.

MOVING BEYOND DESIRE

Spiritual leadership moves us beyond desire. It leads us through stages, and through the gift of the Holy Spirit our devotional practices shape us. We are then led to fruits of the spirit as described by Paul. These disciplines were discussed earlier. It may take days or months to feel this growth taking place. At this time and place that does not matter. What does matter is that we start today with a desire to grow spiritually.

Early in my ministry an older minister told me that I should take advantage of serving a small membership rural church circuit and do more study. I tried to take his advice and do just that.

Admittedly, I enjoy reading. It probably is my favorite pastime. That makes study rather easy. However, I always find that the pressures of work continually squeeze me in other directions. One of the best uses you can make of your particular time and space is to set aside the earliest moments and hours of each day to consciously seek the presence of God. In many ways my rural parish of fewer than three hundred parishioners is less busy than a suburban church of eight hundred members. At the same time, my experience says that ministry seems to expand to fill whatever compassion and energy I am willing and able to give. The important thing is to be intentional about the search for the presence. In every moment and in every space God is working to make the divine presence known to you. In the church that you now serve God is working to make the divine presence known to you. Your spiritual life is the fountain from which your spiritual leadership flows. Make this time and space a blessed moment and place in your journey.

CHAPTER 3

The Small Membership Church as Spiritually Forming Community

THE SETTING

This book began with my memory of an evening spent at Dunkum's Funeral Home. I was there with members of the congregation of the Rocky Mount United Methodist Church. We were mourning the loss of one of the members of that church. The members of Rocky Mount United Methodist Church still gather at Dunkum's to mourn the loss of friends and neighbors. Several years ago I had the privilege of conducting a revival at Rocky Mount. The original building was constructed in 1788. It is still in use. They still have the same organist and the same choir director and the same treasurer they had when I was their pastor more than a third of a century ago. They are still a part of the Buckingham United Methodist Charge.

There have been changes in Rocky Mount, though. Many of the members have died or moved to other places. New members have come into the church. The children who were in my youth group have raised families and in some cases have become grandparents. That 1788 vintage building now has a "new" addition. Rocky Mount has had a number of pastors since my time with them.

My pastoral assignment is now in another place. Earlier I described the setting of my current ministry. In some ways the Burkeville United Methodist Charge is much like the Buckingham United Methodist Charge. In other ways it is quite different. Each pastoral appointment has three churches. Together the appointments have two different spiritual identities. Separately the six churches have six different spiritual identities.

Think of the pastoral assignment you now serve. Consider its unique spiritual identity. If you serve more than one church consider the spiritual identity of each church.

The stages of spiritual development outlined in the first chapter may be helpful to you. The stages are: instinct (feeling), insight (thinking), initiative (doing), integrity (being), and inclusion (sharing). Where is your pastoral appointment in terms of the stages of spiritual growth? Is your appointment a feeling church? How inclusive and hospitable is your church?

One too frequently overlooked spiritual assessment tool is the practice of prayer. Ask God to help you assess the spiritual state of your congregations. Ask God to help you better understand the spiritual journey your church or churches are on. In many ways a spiritual assessment of a parish is more difficult than that of individuals.

THE CHALLENGE

One of the reasons that spiritual assessment of parishes is difficult is that the church is a temporal institution. It is not eternal. Its birth is generally dated to the Pentecost Sunday following the ascension of Jesus (Acts 2). God designed it to be the body of Christ in the world until Christ returns. In many ways it is bound by time and space in ways that other sacred entities are not. The three persons of the Trinity—God the Father, the Son, and the Holy Spirit—for example, are eternal and thus exist beyond time. When we pray we become mystically joined with the eternal.

The church, on the other hand, is perhaps the greatest anchor that God maintains in time and space.

Strangely, though the church is temporal, congregations often seem unchanging. When a church uses a building that dates to 1788 it may appear, in America at least, to be ancient or even eternal. A real danger that all congregations face is that members may assume that the church is eternal and thus take it for granted. Members may assume that their congregation has always been there and will always be there. In truth, since the church is temporal, it follows that each congregation is temporal. This means that congregations, like the buildings in which they worship can die and decay if they are not nurtured as living things. Much of the work of each congregation is done by only a handful of volunteers. This is especially true in a very small church where there are not that many members to begin with.

Our son, Michael, was six years old. His mother was tucking him into bed, and he said to her, "Mom, sometimes I feel like I'm a building and my feelings are too big to get out the door." Perhaps my son's dilemma was similar to that faced by the church for more than two thousand years. The church has been given gifts so large that they are hard to get out of the doors and put into practice. The church is a temporal and finite body housing eternal and infinite gifts. Indeed, even the smallest-membership church is so gifted that it is often impossible for us to live out those gifts inside the community of faith. It is the process of learning how to express our gifts and get them out of the door that is the spiritual journey of the church.

THE JOURNEY

Some pastors and parishioners confuse the physical growth of a church with spiritual growth. They are, in fact, two separate journeys. The physical growth of a church is determined by an increase in the number of people on the membership roll. It can also be measured by things like the number of people attending worship and Sunday school. While it is true that an inclusive spirituality welcomes people, it is not necessarily true that the presence of many people is a sign of inclusive spirituality or spiritual health. Matters of church attendance are always complex. Many factors are involved. Beyond spiritual issues there are things like population size, the number of unchurched people in the area, the proximity of other congregations. The list of factors could go on and on.

The same can be said of financial growth. While it is certainly true that spiritual growth will result in generosity and increased giving to the church, it is not necessarily true that an increase in offerings is a result of increased spiritual growth. As with church attendance, the financial growth of a church is a complex issue. The state of the economy, the economic state of members of a congregation, the economic health of the surrounding community, and many other factors will influence the size of church offerings.

All of the above demonstrate that attempting to assess spiritual growth by an increase in church attendance or offering size is a mistake. It follows that attempts to facilitate spiritual growth through increased church attendance and offering size is also a mistake. Worship attendance and offering size are not necessarily sure indicators of spiritual growth or a means toward spiritual growth. They are, rather, possible outcomes of spiritual growth.

As with the spiritual life of the pastor, the spiritual life of the church is a matter of drawing closer to God. This is done collectively so that the mission of the congregation, the worship, and the program of the church begin to more closely live out the will of God in the life of the Christian community. The spiritual journey of the small membership church also leads to a drawing closer of the members to one another. Love of God and love of neighbor are so interconnected that one cannot happen without the other. First John 4:7-21 is an excellent meditation on this.

THE PARABLE—A GARDEN

Consider Jesus' parable of the Sower (Matt 13:1-9) and its interpretation (Matt 13:18-23). Spiritual leadership in the small membership church is the process of helping the congregation to be formed into a maturing community that draws closer to God. As it does so it produces the fruits of the spirit that Paul refers to (Gal 5:22-23): "love, joy, peace, patience, kindness, generosity, faithfulness, gentleness, and self-control." Think of the church as a garden in which the word of God grows. Think of the congregation as soil in which the word of God grows. Think of your responsibility to help God prepare the hearts of the congregation.

Several weeks ago I saw a colleague who had recently been appointed to a new parish. I asked him about it. He shrugged and said, "It's a church." Remember that just as the sower loves the soil, so God loves the church. No matter the size, each gathering of the body of Christ has a special place in God's heart. One of the dangers of a small membership church assignment is that the pastor may have a feeling of inferiority over the size of the flock. At the same time, concerning my friend's remarks, I think I understand what he meant—all churches share certain characteristics. However, all churches are very different. Just as different individuals and different families have different characteristics, so all congregations have different characteristics.

The pastor of a small membership church was telling me that he sometimes had a difficult time feeling excited about his pastoral appointment. One of his teachers in seminary had been Bishop Desmond Tutu. One day my friend said, "You know if Bishop Tutu were here he would ask me about my appointment. After I described it he would smile and say, 'What a lovely parish!' " Just the memory of Bishop Tutu helped my friend see his parish through his more spiritually mature eyes.

How does a pastor help a church stay focused enough on the sower—God—to produce the hundredfold fruits Jesus spoke about? Consider the parable. The word of God is being sown in your church today. The size of the church makes no difference. As with the spiritual life of the pastor, desire is the first step in preparing the soil of the congregation's heart. The community of faith needs a deep longing to be closer to God.

Recently a friend described a problem facing the church in a pretty graphic way. He said, "Many Christians think of their faith as fire insurance!" The more I pondered his observation the more sense it made. Many churchgoers see our religion as something they do on Sunday to ensure they go to heaven when they die. While it is true that we are promised deliverance from sin and death it is also true that Christianity promises us much more. It promises us a life on earth in which we can experience love, joy, and the very presence of God. It is also true following the analogy of our faith being a fire insurance policy; the premium for the policy has already been paid. Anything owed God for our insurance was paid in full by Jesus' sacrifice on the cross for us.

PREPARING THE SOIL— MEANS OF GRACE

The patient I'm visiting in the hospital is having a rough day. He fusses at me and complains about a number of things. I understand that he has a lot on his mind, yet it is very difficult to deal with him. The nurse, a member of one of my churches, looks at me and smiles. She asks the patient a couple of questions, and he complains to her as he has to me. I know that it is difficult for the nurse to deal with this unhappy patient. Yet, as I watch, she is cheerful and gives him the most loving care possible.

The nurse is a giver of grace. She might be surprised to know that anyone thinks of her that way. Grace is a gift that is undeserved. The patient may not deserve her kindness, but she gives it anyway. That is the kind of person she is.

Many of us fear that God will treat us as we deserve to be treated. If we know ourselves well, that may be cause for fear or worry. The truth is that God is like the nurse. God is the giver of grace.

The word *grace* comes from the Greek word *charis*. It means "favor"—God's favor. It is always given to us as a gift. Grace is manifest in many different ways. Our experience of grace can be placed in several categories. Grace first beckons us. This is our first experience of God. We are called to an awareness of God and invited into God's presence. This form of grace is operative in everyone. When John Wesley was a missionary to Georgia he met Native Americans who influenced his understanding of this type of grace. Though the Native Americans did not know about Christianity, when Wesley spoke to them of God they seemed to be able to grasp the concept and understand God in terms of their own religious experience. Thus, Wesley came to believe that a basic understanding of and experience of God was operative in all people. God is at work in us before we are aware of it. The initial experience of God is primal. This is really the reason that United Methodists baptize babies. We believe their baptism to be an outward sign of God's grace that is operative within infants. Grace exists in all of us long before we are consciously aware of God. It may be understood as a spiritual courtship in which God continually shows us divine love in all sorts of ways. The longer we live with experiences of God's love the more our concept of God takes shape within us. This, too, is a journey.

Later in our spiritual development we experience God through a saving grace that brings awareness of sin and an awareness of the forgiveness of sin. Martin Luther strongly influenced Wesley in understanding this expression of grace. This is the grace that brings us salvation and justifies us before God, to use Luther's terms. In other words this expression of grace brings us into a right relationship with God. This expression of God's grace calls for a response on our part. We accept God's saving love and in turn are given the gift of salvation. Wesley experienced this type of grace at Aldersgate and in the famous passage from his journal wrote of having his heart "strangely warmed."

There is a third expression of grace. This type of grace is experienced as a journey toward holiness. Through this experience of grace we continue to move toward spiritual maturity. It is in this process that we become more Christlike. The experience of this type of grace expresses itself in our spiritual formation. This experience of grace can be understood as a marriage. Using the image of the covenant from Exodus, we move into a relationship with God that can be understood as a marriage covenant. This is an image used in Revelation to describe new Jerusalem—the church—adorned as a bride for God (Rev 21:2).

This discussion of grace is quite simplified. For a fuller understanding you might want to read any of the books available on John Wesley's theology. The "Walk to Emmaus" is a spiritual retreat program for church leaders sponsored by the Upper Room. It does an excellent job of developing this understanding of grace and spiritual formation. In fact, the Walk to Emmaus is one of a group of programs known as "Fourth Day" retreats. These programs started in the Roman Catholic Church and are now conducted in many different denominations. They all do an excellent job of teaching about grace.

Just as God invites individuals into a deeper relationship through grace, so God invites your congregation into a deeper relationship through grace. This deeper relationship may be understood using the stages of spiritual growth outlined in the first chapter. God gives the church several means of grace that will help the congregation mature in spirit and be formed into a loving and hospitable community.

Worship

Attendance at public worship is one of the means of grace available to the church. It is perhaps the most basic. For the community of faith the time and space for gathering are important. In fact, the New Testament word for *church* is *ekklesia*, which means "assembly." Christian discipleship is not a solitary experience. The media today make it easier for people to stay at home and watch televised services. For the person who is homebound or living in a nursing home this is a good thing. For those who are able to get to church and for the congregation itself this is not a good thing. Jesus promised to be present when two or three of his followers gathered (Matt 18:20). When the church gathers it moves beyond time and space and enters the presence of God through Jesus Christ. Almost every Sunday I remind my congregations that I come to church anticipating seeing Jesus.

Worship is both a private and a public expression of our response to God's grace, and it is a wonderful tool for our use in turning the heart of the small membership church into the good soil that can better know and respond to God's presence. Many good people say things like: "I'm a Christian, but my relationship with God is private—just between us" or "I really don't see the need to go to church as long as I try to do what is right and be a good person." These statements miss the point of worship, and miss much of the central meaning of the Christian faith.

Again, Jesus teaches us that he is present within the gathered community of faith. Unlike some other religions, Christianity is a communal religion. The church has always understood itself to be the body of Christ in the world. It is only logical that Christians should meet together to seek a closer relationship with God and to seek a greater awareness of God's presence within their lives, within their community, and within the congregation.

When planning a worship service the pastor needs to stay focused on the goal of worship. Using the parable of the Sower, the goal is always a harvest. As the one who plans and conducts the worship service the pastor acts as a partner with God in the sowing of seed. This is often an especially burdensome responsibility for the small membership church pastor who must do the work with no other professional help. When you have a staff to help coordinate worship the end product can come out of the dynamics of the staff working together. The small membership church pastor often works alone in a study or office with only God as a partner. Even the task of printing and folding worship bulletins may fall into the lap of the pastor. Recently I heard of one pastor who would take unfolded bulletins to church every Sunday and have the first people to arrive fold them. If you do not have a church staff it is important that you allow members to share responsibilities in putting together worship in as many ways as possible. Even with volunteers helping, the factors mentioned make worship planning time and energy consuming.

It is essential that the pastor start with a devotional life centered in God. The worship experience of the congregation on Sunday morning must flow out of the pastor's spiritual journey. The pastor also needs to draw on the spiritual life of the congregation in order to put together the worship service. At this point

39

it is helpful for the pastor to realize that all congregations have some spiritual things in common. Worship services, though always tailored to meet the needs of specific congregations, should include key elements that are needed by all congregations. These include: praise, proclamation, and response. In order for the small membership church to move toward a deeper relationship with God the worship service must help deepen the soil of the congregation's heart.

Each Sunday worship service is like a family reunion. Whatever problems a church may have, it is generally the time of gathering that is most joyful. In the small membership church this may be especially true. In fact, the smaller the membership the more likely people are to know each other and to know each other well. As members gather they share spiritual concerns. This begins long before the prelude is played. It begins when people first step onto the church grounds. Simple conversation begins about the health and welfare of aged parents, issues involving childrearing and parenting, and other personal issues that have deep spiritual dimensions. As the community begins to gather they seek God and begin to experience God through the care and compassion and, indeed, the very presence of brothers and sisters in the congregation. The pastor can call attention to this during the sermon or in conversation with members. In so doing the pastor helps members understand the deep spiritual and pastoral quality of relationships within God's family.

It is important to have greeters in your church. These need to be people who are friendly and approachable. They need to be people who welcome all who enter the doors of the church. What keeps people returning to church is a feeling of belonging. The coming together and feeling good about being together also meet the emotional and instinctual needs of Christians—all Christians. Church members need to feel loved and accepted.

As church members move into the church they are confronted with a cross and an altar. These are tangible reminders of the sacrifice and real presence of Christ. In most churches the building is designed so that members face the altar and the cross during the entire service. Members are literally taking their lives individually and as a family of faith and putting them within the context of God's presence and Christ's sacrifice for all people. This is a powerful symbol, and it is made even more powerful in a small membership congregation where people know each other intimately. Ushers and acolytes are very important in establishing the right environment in which spiritual soil is deepened for the congregation. The ushers meet people and lead them toward the altar. The acolyte in a literal way brings light, thus reminding the members of the presence of God and the illumination it brings. An advantage youth and adults have in small membership churches is that all of them may have an opportunity to serve as acolytes and ushers. In a larger church many members never have an opportunity to serve in these capacities.

Now consider the parts of the worship service and the way they are designed to heighten awareness of the presence of God in the midst of the congregation. Consider how the parts of the service are designed to shape our thoughts and meditations so that they are more focused on preparing the soil for the presence of God.

The most common element in public worship is perhaps praise. Praise is often referred to as adoration. Most worship services begin with praise. A moving prelude, an invocation, or a call to worship normally express praise to God. These elements are often followed by a hymn of praise. All of these acts of praise are done within the context of the gathered body of Christ to remind all of us that we praise God together. Having the congregation responsively read a psalm is an especially effective way to build the good soil of a deeper spirituality. Reading the Scriptures together as a call to worship is a communal act of faith. It involves the entire congregation in praise together. Singing a hymn of praise together has a similar effect. Acts of praise reflect the wonder and awe we feel when we sense the divine presence. They remind us that God chooses to enter into our time and space. It is God's nature and God's way to enter into our community in an active and powerful way. Indeed, as James 4:8 reminds us, as we draw close to God, God draws near to us.

Acts of proclamation are central to all worship. The gathered community proclaims God's acts and presence in our lives and in our history in various ways. Confession is one of the most powerful. This is especially true in small congregations where the people are all too often very aware of the sin and brokenness in each life and in the life of the church. This makes confession much more painful at times, but it also makes it more healing and dynamic. Typically, congregations go to God in silent individual confession and then join in praying a prayer of confession together. Following the prayers of confession the minister proclaims pardon and absolution. Taken as a whole these acts of confession and pardon humbly express our shared need for forgiveness and greater dependence on God. They then proclaim the power of God's reconciling love. When done as a community, they are reminders that all of us together share in the brokenness we call sin and the glory we call salvation. God has acted, and continues to act in Jesus Christ to forgive all our sins and grant us eternal life.

Proclamation reaches its high point in worship in the reading of Scripture and delivery of the sermon. Many worship services have the assembled congregation share in the readings through reading responsively. This allows everyone in attendance to actively participate in proclamation of the good news of the Scriptures. Having a lay reader read the lessons is also an effective way to involve the community, thus producing deeper soil. One weakness many modern churches have is that members no longer bring their own Bibles to church. I encourage members to bring Bibles, but our churches also provide pew Bibles. In our worship bulletins we always include the pew Bible page number of the Scripture lesson and then give people the opportunity to follow along. This not only gets them involved in the sacred act of proclamation, but it also familiarizes the people with how it feels to hold and read God's word.

Many churches follow the liturgical year and use the Revised Common Lectionary. Earlier the use of the lectionary in the spiritual formation of the pastor was discussed. The lectionary is a group of readings that follow a three-year cycle and touch on most of the major themes of the Bible. Each Sunday has three lessons in the lectionary. These lessons normally come from the Old Testament or Hebrew Scriptures, an epistle or letter from the New Testament, and a reading from one of the Gospels, again from the New Testament. The lectionary is, however, more than a list of suggested Scripture lessons. It is also a celebration of the events of the church year. The year begins four weeks before Christmas with the season of Advent. This is a time of preparation for the coming of God's son, Jesus, into our time and space. The events around Christmas are celebrated with the seasons of Advent, Christmas, and Epiphany. The other main event of the church year is Easter. It is a celebration of the resurrection. This celebration begins with a six-week observance of Lent. It is a time of penance and cleansing as the church prepares for Easter. Lent ends with Holy Week during which Jesus' crucifixion is celebrated. Following Holy Week the church celebrates the resurrection on Easter Sunday. When we share in this celebration together as a community we are reminded of the victory of all of God's people over sin and the grave. The season of Easter continues for seven weeks and is followed by Pentecost. This season celebrates the giving of the Holy Spirit to the church. This celebration is the story of the birth of the church, and is a reminder that the presence of the Holy Spirit is a gift to the church.

Worshiping as a community allows us to see our individual lives within the context of the story of our faith. I remember a time when I was struggling with some personal things and was becoming very angry and bitter. I shared my troubles with a good friend who listened and then asked me to reflect on my suffering within the context of Christ's suffering for me. This took place at the beginning of Lent and for the next six weeks I consciously prayed and meditated on this. I asked God to help me understand my own suffering within the context of Jesus' suffering for me, and it made a difference. I was able to take my suffering to church and think, pray, and meditate on it as a part of the suffering community. I was able to do this as I heard the story of Christ's suffering retold through the worship services I attended. It helped me see my own troubles within a different perspective and healing began to take place. The healing better helped me feel the presence of the God who is truly with me and within the church at all times.

The sermon is designed to proclaim the Scriptures by interpreting and applying them to the issues we face in our own lives. The sermon provides a kind of nurture through allowing us to reflect on our lives and the meaning of the Scriptures. The sermon helps make good soil by reminding the members of the congregation of how the Scriptures speak to the issues faced by the congregation and world.

Proclamation is followed by response. The assembled congregation responds with things like an affirmation of faith, the presentation of an offering and prayers, or other acts of thanksgiving. These responses also include Holy Communion. These acts of response allow us to put into words and actions our faith that God is present within the life of the community.

Each Sunday is a "little Easter" because it is a celebration of the resurrection in the life of the church. It is a time when God's acts of love and redemption are reenacted within the community of faith. Attending public worship gives us the opportunity to begin the week in a way that will deepen our spiritual soil by focusing our thoughts on the presence of God.

Holy Communion

Holy Communion is one of the church's most important means of grace. Sometimes small membership churches have not benefited from receiving Holy Communion on a frequent or regular basis. In most churches only ordained clergy administer Holy Communion. Many small membership churches exist in rural areas where historically it has been difficult to have ordained clergy available at all times. Thus, many of our churches may be used to receiving Holy Communion on a quarterly or even more infrequent basis. This is not good for the church. Every church needs to gather around the Lord's Table as frequently as possible.

Consider Holy Communion and the way it makes for richer soil in the heart of your congregation.

Experiencing the presence of God always starts as an act of divine grace. It always begins with a choice on God's part. God wants us to know the divine presence as an ongoing reality in our daily lives. God wants our small membership churches to know the divine presence in their daily lives. This means that God's presence is much more than what we experience through worship, prayer, and meditation. It means that God is with us while we are doing even the most routine chores. In the sacrament of Holy Communion we encounter God in unique and beautiful ways in our time and space.

Many of us have had the experience of suddenly becoming aware of God's love while doing some routine activity. Surely God is there all the time but suddenly God becomes real in unexpected ways. It is possible to increase our sensitivity to the presence so that we are often consciously aware of God as a real and powerful part of our lives at every moment. Holy Communion is a deep expression of desire on God's part. It is a celebration of God's giving of the divine self to us. Receiving Holy Communion is a response on our part to an action on God's part.

Different churches have different beliefs and practices around the celebration of Holy Communion. Beliefs range from seeing it as a symbolic event to actually believing that the bread and wine are changed into the blood and body of Christ during the celebration. Practices range from open communion in which all people present are invited to participate to closed communion in which only certain people—usually members of the congregation—are welcomed. As mentioned above, churches also differ in how frequently Holy Communion is served. Some churches celebrate Holy Communion as a part of weddings and funerals.

The Wesleyan understanding of Holy Communion is that it is a sacrament. This means that it is an act that goes back to Jesus. Wesleyans also believe that it is an act in which we are nurtured and fed. In other words, it is an act through which the soil of the heart of a congregation is deepened and enriched. This act is more than a memorial. A memorial is simply a memory. Holy Communion is also a mysterious act in which Jesus Christ is somehow uniquely present. Since Jesus promised to always be present when two or three of us are gathered, we believe Jesus to be present at all gatherings for worship. To worship is to enter the presence of Jesus Christ. We believe Jesus to be present at an even deeper level as we receive Holy Communion.

All four Gospels give an account of the institution of Holy Communion. These are found in Matthew 26:26-29, Mark 14:22-25, Luke 22:14-23, and John 14–17. John's account is very different. Rather than actually giving the disciples bread and wine and telling them to continue to celebrate his presence through this act, Jesus gives them a long teaching about abiding in him. Paul passes on to us the importance of Holy Communion in 1 Corinthians 11:23-26. In so doing he is giving us the first-century teachings and traditions that he knew. He tells us that as often as we receive the bread and wine we proclaim Jesus' death and resurrection until he comes again. The account of the journey to Emmaus in Luke 24:13-35 may well be based in the celebration of Holy Communion. In that story the resurrected Jesus travels with followers on the road to Emmaus but is not recognized until he breaks and blesses bread at a table with them. All these Scriptures point to the importance of this act. They remind us that the celebration of Holy Communion anchors the church into the life of Jesus' death, resurrection, and return.

To understand more about Holy Communion we must consider its context. It is generally celebrated within the gathered community of faith. The gathered body of Christ celebrates his death and resurrection through this act. It is also done within the context of confession and affirmation. As we approach the table we confess our sins. The act of confession acknowledges our dependence on God's grace and forgiveness. We confess our sins and we receive pardon from the God of grace. We often affirm our faith through a formal affirmation. The most ancient affirmations we have are the Apostles' Creed and the Nicene Creed. Through reciting one of these creeds together we join the rest of the gathered family of God in stating our faith publicly. It is within this context of confession and affirmation that we receive Holy Communion. In this setting we then receive the presence of the one who died and rose again for us. Receiving is actually an act of thanks. In fact, the prayer in which the bread and wine are consecrated is known as the Great Thanksgiving. This prayer and the sacrament itself acknowledge our thanks to God for what has been done for us in the sacrifice of Jesus Christ for our sin and for the sin of the world. In this sense, it not only grounds the congregation in the life of God, but it also grounds them in the life of the world.

Much of this appears to us as mysterious and perhaps confusing. In fact, many services of Holy Communion state *the mystery of faith:* "Christ has died; Christ is risen; Christ will come again." This affirmation, while acknowledging the mystery that surrounds the acts of God's love toward us, focuses our thoughts on the past (Christ has died), present (Christ is risen), and future (Christ will come again). These simple statements remind us that all of our time is somehow swallowed up by eternity in Christ's actions for us. This part of Holy Communion points beyond this time and place and reminds us that the very meaning of our lives is found in eternity. We are reminded that in the celebration of Holy Communion the eternal is present in our time and space—within the life of the community of faith. The Holy is thus experienced as present in the life of the church. No matter how small the church, it contains the life of the Holy. This act reminds the church of who we are and whose we are. We are a people redeemed by the sacrifice of our Lord, Jesus Christ.

Bible Study

Another means of grace that is necessary for the spiritual development of the small membership church is Bible study. Nothing does more to make good soil of our hearts and spirits than Bible study. In fact, in Jesus' parable the seed is the word of

God. Bible study focuses our thoughts on God in a unique way. It causes awareness of God to sprout and grow within our hearts and spirits individually and collectively in remarkable ways. If any conscious and intentional act can prepare our spirits for a greater awareness of the divine presence, study of the writings that we consider the very word of God is the logical place to start.

The small membership church lends itself to Bible study in several ways. Small membership churches have a kind of social intimacy that comes from everyone knowing everyone else at a deep level. That kind of intimacy is invaluable in the dynamics of a small group of disciples who come together weekly to study the Bible. They often come together having already established a high level of trust. The small size of the group makes it much less intimidating for many people to ask questions. The small size of the group tends to provide more people with time to ask questions.

It helps move the group to an even deeper level of intimacy and trust when the leader models humility and acceptance. Part of this is done through an open admission that the leader does not have complete knowledge of the Bible. Many church members are very embarrassed at their lack of knowledge of Scriptures. Over the years a number of parishioners have told me that they are afraid to try to follow along in reading the Scripture lessons during Sunday worship because they are so unfamiliar with the Bible that they will fumble through pages without ever finding the lesson.

Most people do not find the Bible easy to understand. Perhaps the best way of helping a congregation study the Bible is by trying to lead them to a greater awareness of what the Bible is. As mentioned above, the church has always believed it to be the word of God. That means that we consider the Bible to be inspired by God. The church has always believed the Bible contains all the truth necessary to experience God and obtain salvation. But what exactly is the Bible?

The Bible is the church's book. The process of writing and eventually naming the writings of the Bible as authoritative—the word *canonical* is used for sacred texts and means "measuring-stick"—was done by the church. In fact, the congregations in which the Gospels and Epistles were written and the congregations to which they were written may have been no larger than the congregations you and I serve. That means that they were originally and intentionally written for an audience like ours. It is often helpful to remind your group of this.

The Bible is actually more a library than a single book. It was written over a period of many years. It is a record of how people experienced God in their history and in their hopes. It is many different kinds of literature. Some of the books are history, some are poetry, and some are prayers or hymns. They were originally written in Hebrew, Greek, and Aramaic and only translated into our language, English, in the last five centuries. It is fortunate that today we have many good and reliable translations of the Bible available to us. I encourage the members of our Bible Study group to bring to our study the version of the Bible they are most comfortable with. When there is a difference in the wording of different versions we talk about what the words mean in the original Greek or Hebrew. We read aloud, each person reading a verse from his or her Bible and then moving on to the next person. As people feel comfortable with the sound of their voice it seems to make asking and answering questions easier for them.

Two of the churches I serve have joined together for their Bible study and they are currently studying the Gospel of Luke. Each week I begin by asking what type of literature—or what genre—Luke is. When someone tells me it is a Gospel I ask the class what *Gospel* means. This is all very basic, but I believe it helps build trust and openness to begin each session with simple things that everyone in the group knows and can respond to. As the discussion becomes more complex I am very careful to be open and accepting of the answers that people give to my questions. There is usually some part of each answer that I can affirm. When I am asked questions I often toss them back to the group and ask them what they think. After much discussion in which many people participate I tell them what other scholars and theologians have said about the passage. We often talk about how the theme or the narrative of our study material relates to our lives. This helps members integrate the teachings of the Scriptures not only into their lives but into the life of the congregation. It's not unusual for people to come to Bible study in great anticipation, their minds full of questions they can't wait to ask. If you are not comfortable with this type of Bible study, there are many excellent programs available through all denominations. Two United Methodist resources, *Disciple* and *Companions in Christ,* are quite different and they offer two very distinct ways of studying the Bible.

How is the congregation to read and study the Bible? Several things need to happen. Earlier I discussed the reading of the Bible in worship. Christians also should be encouraged to read in their private devotions. If the congregation follows the Revised Common Lectionary there are several excellent devotional books that also follow the lectionary. They help the congregation to see their devotions within the larger context of communal worship and the celebration of the church year. Some people will want to read the Bible completely through from cover to cover. There are excellent Bibles available that are divided so that over a period of one year the entire Bible can be read. There are also many excellent study Bibles available. These can be quite helpful for Christians who want to learn more about the texts.

Prayer

Another means of grace available to the small membership church is prayer. Prayer is so basic to the spiritual life that we may perhaps take it for granted. The congregation may want to do a study on prayer. The congregation may form prayer circles. The congregation may have a prayer chain. The congregation certainly prays when it gathers on Sunday. God listens to and answers prayer. Psalm 37:4 tells us that if we delight in God, God will give us the desires of our heart. All of us have an awareness of the presence of God as a divine gift. This awareness can grow, but such growth must come as a result of desire on our part. This is true of individuals as well as congregations.

Consider the parable of the Garden. Desire is always our first step in preparing the soil of our hearts and spirits so that our very lives—individually and as a congregation—become the good soil in which the very presence of God may grow. Once we have the desire, how do we respond?

The response of desire must be followed by a conscious attempt on our part to communicate that desire to God. The most basic form of this communication is prayer. Countless volumes have been written on prayer. Studies show that most Americans believe in the power of prayer. Earlier the importance of praise was discussed. A great mystic once wrote that prayers of praise are the most important type of prayer. She believed that we should spend half of our prayer time in praise. This sounds simple but many of us—individually and as congregations—do not know how to use prayer time as a time of praise. The Psalms can be a good place to start looking for examples of prayers of praise. Psalm 150, for example, almost explodes off the pages of the Bible as a verbal fireworks display in celebration of God's glory and goodness. It ends the book of Psalms as Americans end the Fourth of July, with a display of glorious noise and awesome wonder. Reading through the Psalms will reveal many phrases of praise that can be incorporated in our prayers. In fact, the Psalms themselves are prayers. The Lord's Prayer starts with the theme of praise—"hallowed be thy name." Praise prepares our hearts for a deeper awareness of the presence by focusing on the gratitude we feel for God's goodness.

Intercession is another form of prayer that is essential to the spiritual growth of a congregation. Intercession is praying for God's involvement in the cares and concerns of others. Remembering to pray for others moves us outward from the heart to ever-growing circles of love and concern for others—our family, friends, the church, those in need around the world. Prayer for enemies can do much to shape our hearts and deepen the soil of our spirits. A church member who is well on his way to spiritual maturity told our Bible study group that he had a coworker who was a constant source of conflict. The church member is a recovering addict, and when he told his rehabilitation counselor about this person, the counselor told him to begin to pray for the man. Although it was hard to do, my friend prayed for the individual daily. Eventually, the two men began to be able to work together without conflict. It is difficult to hold on to negative feelings about another person when we remember to pray for them. Enemies do not have to be people. During my ordination sermon the bishop said that our enemies might be things like a copy machine or a car. Enemies can be anything or anyone we see as a threat to our happiness or well-being.

An important part of our worship service is the sharing of prayer concerns. With us, this time of sharing sometimes goes on for fifteen or twenty minutes. The congregation mentions people and things that they want to include in the pastoral prayer. As people share these joys and concerns the whole congregation seems to form an intimacy among themselves and with God. This period of sharing leads into a period of silent prayer in which spoken and unspoken concerns are prayed.

Korean Christians use a form of prayer called Tongsung Kido. This is a congregational form of prayer in which all of the people pray a petition aloud. Rather than praying in unison, each member of the congregation prays in the way the Holy Spirit directs him or her. Together their voices swell and fill the sanctuary. After a time the pastor begins the pastoral prayer. This can be a most powerful form of congregational prayer. The individual voices and prayers seem to become one.

In discussing worship we discussed confession. It is important that the congregation pray a prayer of confession together. Sin is not only individual; it is communal. After a communal prayer of confession the pastor offers words of absolution. Together the community is forgiven and restored. This act of prayer is a most important way of building the spirit of a congregation.

Prayers of intercession for the church are very important. This is different from intercessions for individual members. It means prayers for the body of Christ as a congregation or as a part of the larger church. When prayers are prayed for the body the individual concerns begin to fall away and the individual members find themselves lost in the context of bigger issues and concerns.

Earlier I mentioned that I have set aside one day a week to focus my prayers and devotions on each of my churches. I pray for Ward's Chapel on Mondays, Bethel on Tuesdays, and Salem on Wednesdays. I have shared this with the people and encouraged them to join in setting aside one day a week to pray for their church.

Spiritual Friendship

Spiritual friendship is yet another means of grace. Members are encouraged to meet on a regular basis for prayer and sharing. Sometimes this is done formally through groups like Companions in Christ or other small groups. It is also done when members covenant to meet weekly or on some other regular schedule for prayer and sharing. Two members can meet for coffee or breakfast once a week. Through this type of sharing the spiritual growth of the congregation deepens.

In one community women from many small membership churches meet for a monthly prayer breakfast. This group crosses racial and denominational lines. They meet at a restaurant one Sunday morning each month. The meeting is announced in all of their churches and is open to all who wish to attend.

Two men from the same small membership church become prayer partners. They covenant to pray for each other. They meet at least weekly to share morning coffee and talk about spiritual things.

Small mission groups have gone from our area to Russia and parts of the Caribbean. These groups have helped participants bond at a deep level. From that experience men and women have continued to share their spiritual journeys.

The Walk to Emmaus program was mentioned earlier. Emmaus encourages people to enter some sort of covenant group. How the group functions is shaped by the needs of the people who form it. The important thing is that the participants come together with a willingness to support one another in prayer. They also support their churches in prayer.

In all of these instances spiritual friendship reminds people that they are not alone. Spiritual friendship provides an opportunity to share our spiritual journey with others.

Deeds of Kindness and Mercy

Deeds of kindness and mercy are basic to the life of the Christian congregation. They are also essential to the building of the spiritual soil of the congregation. These acts are the church in mission. Though our churches are small in terms of membership, they are large in terms of involvement in the community and world. As I write this our United Methodist Men are involved in the renovation of the home of an elderly widow in the community, several of our teens just finished a mission camp in which they repaired a home and gleaned vegetables for the hungry. In one of the churches I currently serve one woman has brought the church alive through her work as missions coordinator. She has started having our children collecting money and aluminum cans for missions. The children also collect pocket change in a "march of pennies" collection each Sunday. This money goes to various charities including St. Jude's Children's Research Hospital. She has also organized two large yard sales each year. The money collected there all goes to missions. Additionally leftover items are donated to local shelters. In addition to all of that, she has had the church put together care packages for our service members deployed overseas. The possibilities of good works that a small membership church can be involved in are virtually endless. When the congregation looks toward others it looks beyond its own walls and interests. This is necessary to fulfill Jesus' command to serve the world.

Several of the spiritual disciplines as means of grace were considered above. Through worship, receiving Holy Communion, Bible study, prayer, spiritual friendship, and deeds of mercy and kindness a small membership congregation will find its spiritual soil enriched. It will find itself moving closer to God. If these practices are done in a disciplined way the congregation will be more sensitive to the presence of God.

THE DESIRE TO BLESS

Just as pastors must learn to bless their own lives and experiences, so congregations must learn to bless their own lives. Once they become comfortable with who they are and with the uniqueness of their journey they become much more ready and able to bless others by extending to them hospitality and love. Your congregation is on a unique faith journey. It is blessed. It is a journey toward holiness. It is a journey toward God.

Perhaps your limitations make the journey seem like a trek through the desert. Remember that the Bible tells a story of how remarkable things happen in a desert. The journey of the Hebrews to the promised land caused them to question God's ability to provide for them. Their question is poetically told in Psalm 78:19-20: "Can God spread a table in the wilderness? / Even though he struck the rock so that water gushed out / and torrents overflowed, / can he also . . . provide meat for his people?" The answer to their question is answered poetically in Psalm 107:35: "He turns a desert into pools of water, / a parched land into springs of water." The question is also answered in Luke 9:12-17. Here Jesus feeds the crowd of five thousand in the desert.

The above scriptures give witness that we do not have to own plenty or be in an ideal place to experience God's abundance. God gives to us in the desert. What is important is not where we are or what we have. What is important is that we desire to find God in this moment. What matters is that we, the church, desire to love and praise God in this moment. What matters is that we realize that God is with us in the desert. No matter what challenges our church faces, no matter how few our resources, God provides. We desire the blessing, and we desire to use the blessing that God gives to us to bless others.

Churches are often asked to participate in local parades or festivals. One small membership church's youth group made a float for a harvest festival parade. The youth built the float and rode on it. They decided that a dove of peace was a good symbol for their church. The float featured a beautiful white dove made out of chicken wire and tissue paper. The creativity, smiles, and music of the youth told the community of their desire to be a blessing. The work that the young people did also helped focus their own spirits on their desire to bless.

MOVING BEYOND DESIRE

Spiritual leadership moves the small membership congregation beyond desire. Through the gift of the Holy Spirit its devotional practices transform it. The congregation moves through stages. It moves from feelings to a place of inclusion. It moves from having its own needs met to reaching out to meet the needs of the community and the world.

Congregations move through stages toward spiritual maturity in much the same way that individuals do. As with individuals, often the change is so gradual that members are not aware that it is taking place.

CHAPTER 4

Roadblocks to the Journey

The church was having a conflict management class. Sam volunteered to role-play. Off the top of my head I thought of a rather silly situation to have him act out. I asked him to arrive at the church on Christmas Eve and discover that the Christmas tree he had cut and set up in the church had been thrown out and replaced by a bigger tree. Sam really got into the role. He played it with a lot of anger and frustration. After the class I told him I really appreciated the way he put himself into the role and made the situation come alive. He was still a bit angry and said, "That wasn't play! That thing really happened to me here several years ago!" I was shocked. My intent was to use a perfectly innocent, silly situation to illustrate how we deal with conflict. Unknowingly, I had dreamed up a situation that was neither innocent nor silly to Sam.

The life of the church is often filled with conflict. There are certainly different kinds of conflict. Some conflict may seem silly or innocent. Other conflict may seem serious and evil. In this chapter we will consider several types of conflict that are typically part of congregational life.

INNER CONFLICT

All of us have inner conflict. Inner conflict is a sickness of the soul. Both churches and individuals experience it. Where the church gathers there is inner conflict. Paul wrote about inner conflict in Romans 7:18-20: "For I know that nothing good dwells within me, that is, in my flesh. I can will what is right, but I cannot do it. For I do not do the good I want, but the evil I do not want is what I do. Now if I do what I do not want, it is no longer I that do it, but sin that dwells within me." Paul's problem is our problem in many ways. How often do we find ourselves unable to do the things we want? How often do we find ourselves doing what we know to be wrong as disciples of Jesus? This leads to inner conflict.

A woman says to me, "I keep trying to be better. If you knew what I was really like inside you wouldn't like me, either. You see, I like the bright lights and the glitter."

A young man comes to see me. He is due to be transferred to a job in another state and has just discovered that his mother has cancer and the doctor says she doesn't have long to live. He knows that he is running out of time—time to deal with his boss, time to say good-bye to his mother.

Another woman tells me that she often feels bewildered by the turns that her life takes. She says she often looks up and says to God, "OK, you've got my attention. Now there must be a reason for this."

Years ago I knew a man who would put his hands over his head whenever he entered the church. He would look upward and pretend to ask God not to strike him with lightning for entering a holy place. He did it as sort of a joke, but he was probably dealing with something that really bothers a lot of people. Many of us feel unworthy to come before God. It is hard for us to speak to God, to pray, or to go to worship.

Many of us go through life feeling that God is *out to get us* for the mistakes we have made. The last thing that we want to do is try to speak to God or to seek God's presence. What my friend joked about—fear that God will punish him—may not be a joking matter in his mind.

A young man sits up in his bed and says to me, "I wonder why I got sick. I think God is punishing me."

A fellow pastor talks about his parishioners operating on the edge of their resources. For them life is often a matter of feeling so overwhelmed that they hope they have the time and energy left to do what they need to do for themselves and their families. Days bring pressure, days bring sadness, days bring challenges— ready or not!

Many of us may come to church each week to find the kind of simple answers to life's meaning that will keep us from being over our heads as we try our best to live out our Christian faith each day. Yet, many of us sadly face Monday morning quickly feeling overwhelmed. We feel over our heads the first time we realize that our boss is going to yell at us, that we are too tired to run an errand that must be run, that we do not know how to say, "I'm sorry" to one whose feelings we have hurt. Our cry may be, "Lord, help me to survive, to understand, to know how to live with the faith that you are here with me." The truth is that we live in a very real world of confusing messages, moral dilemmas, and frustrated hopes.

Though much of our inner conflict is self-inflicted, there are those whose pain goes much deeper. Little Eddie's mother was a single parent. She couldn't afford day care, so she left him in a town one hundred miles away. He lived with relatives. About once every four or six weeks she would take the bus to see him on Saturday afternoon. The bus arrived at 2:00. Little Eddie would be so excited every Saturday that he would run to meet the bus. He knew, though, that his mother might not be on it, so to protect himself from disappointment he would wait for the bus on a distant hill where he could watch the bus stop. If his mother got off the bus he would run to meet her. If she did not get off, then Little Eddie would turn, and with tears in his eyes, wander off alone to cry. At least three weeks out of the month she was not there for him.

And sometimes even when parents are there physically, they are not there emotionally or spiritually. Little Sally remembers the night she took her mother to a Girl Scout banquet. It was a mother-daughter event, and Sally was very proud of the dinner she prepared for her mother until she placed it in front of her mother only to hear her mother make fun of it and complain loudly about how bad it tasted. Sally remembers ducking her head, and being too embarrassed to look to either side as she ate her own meal in silence.

All of these stories are true. They were all told to me by the little ones who lived them. And all of these little ones are now between forty-five and fifty-five years old. As I listen to the stories of their childhoods I feel that I am not listening to adults looking back at painful memories, but rather to sad little ones who still feel neglected, abused, unappreciated, unloved, and hindered by others who were not there for them spiritually or emotionally. This, too, caused inner conflict. It follows that the more we feel in conflict with ourselves, the more difficult it becomes to hear God's call in our lives and in the life of the church. Inner conflict within the individual can also hurt the church. If we are angry about our past, this anger can come out inappropriately in committee meetings, it might come out as angry teasing that drives others away from a church that they see as unkind. When we become defensive during fellowship this causes those around us to become uncomfortable. This causes inner conflict within the body of the church.

There are many ways in which the church has inner conflict. Earlier we discussed how we are pulled into different directions by the demands and messages of the world around us. Most of us have far too many things to do. It is true of individuals and of the entire congregation. Wondering how to set priorities causes inner conflict. All churches worry about money. The small membership church may struggle with knowing that handicapped people can not climb the steps and yet knowing that they do not have enough money to buy an elevator. Some churches have inner conflict over watching a neighboring church grow in membership and wondering why they remain small. Feelings of inferiority over the condition of the church building may hinder the congregation's ability to bless.

Balance is necessary in dealing with inner conflict. Finding a balance is difficult, and when we feel things are not balanced we feel guilty and experience inner conflict. In the church we may feel torn between the need to feed the poor of the community, send our youth to camp, and pay the electric bill. Members may feel guilty because they do not seem to have time for Wednesday night prayer meeting or because they do not believe they can afford to tithe.

Several months ago the chair of our administrative council approached me after a meeting. In my report I had talked about several spiritual formation programs that were available for the people. Several other council members mentioned vital ministries they are involved in. The chair noted that none of these ministries or programs even received comment from the people in attendance. The one topic that had generated energy and heated discussion was whether or not to remove an old tree from the church yard. Think about what the church is in conflict about.

What are the attitudes of the churches you serve? Would members of your church like to invite a friend of a different race to worship with them, but are not sure of the welcome they would receive? Recently a pastor told me that one of her church members works at a shelter for battered women. One day this member was combing the hair of a beautiful African American four-year-old girl when the child's mother asked if she knew where she could take her daughter to Sunday school. My friend's church member felt ashamed that she didn't offer to bring her to her own church, but she didn't want to expose a family that had already suffered abuse and rejection to what might turn out to be a chilly reception. Do we trust the church to be a place of love and refuge to all people?

A former member stopped attending church for several years because she was so ashamed that her daughter became pregnant and "had to" get married. Do we trust the church to be a place of love in all situations? This lack of trust causes inner conflict.

INTRAFAMILY CONFLICT

A man comes to see me. He has a young teenage son who has run away from home. The boy is now safely back home, but my friend says, "I just want to get things fixed up before his life gets ruined. I don't want him to repeat the mistakes that I made when I was his age. If I'm part of the problem, I want to help." He's a loving father who is afraid that he is running out of time and answers.

A couple comes to see me. He has been unfaithful one too many times. She says to me, "I've run out of patience. I can't forgive him again! It's finished!" Too often forgiveness and patience are taken for granted or interpreted as weakness and we find ourselves taken advantage of by friends or family. We, too, run out of patience.

Families often fight. Family violence is now recognized as a serious problem within our society. Families often separate. The divorce rate in our nation remains high. Sometimes family conflict takes place over a period of generations. Church members, being human, are not immune to family conflict. Whatever conflict is going on within families is brought into the church. People take sides. It frequently becomes church conflict. In order to be dealt with it must be recognized for what it is.

Intrafamily conflict involving large extended families is also a major problem for many small membership churches. When I first arrived at the Buckingham United Methodist Charge I asked one of the former pastors for advice. He asked for a sheet of paper. On the top of it he wrote three family names. He said, "Your church membership is made up of these three families. They are in all three churches. If this page were big enough I would outline how they are all related to each other. Just remember that they are all kin. When there is conflict within any of these three families it will somehow get played out in the church. Also remember that you are the outsider." During the four years I served that appointment I often thought about my friend's words. They were not really advice. They were really just words of wisdom. His insight into those churches holds true about the makeup of my current parish. I have several large families that make up a significant part of the church's membership.

Though not healthy or ideal, intrafamily conflict is a part of congregational life in the small membership church. Do not expect church members to become saints who are able to put their conflicts behind them when they come to church for a committee meeting or worship service.

This type of conflict may be expressed in a variety of ways. Conflicts over money, conflicts of power or perceived power within the church, conflicts over mission priorities, conflicts over matters of ethics, and communication problems are just a few examples. In fact, just about any conflict within the congregation may have its roots in intrafamily struggles.

INTERFAMILY CONFLICT

There are often conflicts between families. The dynamics of this are similar to those of intrafamily conflict. In fact, when families intermarry a mixture of intrafamily and interfamily conflict may result. Painful as this may be, it too is often just a part of the baggage that church members bring with them when they come to church.

Two families in a small membership church have been fighting for over a century. They live on adjoining farms. There have been arguments between them over issues involving right of way through property, road and fence maintenance, and water usage. The men in these two families do not like each other. Several members from both families sit together on committees. Is it a surprise that they argue and find themselves in conflict while trying to do church business? Their personal and professional baggage separates them and often spreads beyond the two families and leads to larger conflict within the church.

CULTURAL AND RACIAL CONFLICT

One of the most destructive forms of conflict encountered within the small membership church is racial conflict. In many areas churches remain largely racially segregated. Though this is changing, it is still an issue for many small membership churches.

Indeed, the fact that much of the membership of a small church may come from one, two, or several families may encourage racial segregation. A church made up of three families may tend to attract mostly members of those families. It may be extremely difficult for a church to look beyond racial issues that separate people. Some church members may strongly resist inclusion of people of different races or ethnic backgrounds in church membership or church functions.

Unfortunately racial conflict may mask itself as something different. Some people have learned that it is not acceptable to admit to feelings of racial prejudice. This type of problem is often difficult to deal with because it is not expressed openly.

Many people may have racial prejudice simply because the church has not made *inclusion* as big an issue as Jesus' teachings make it. Recently I was surprised when a church member admitted to me that he had feelings of racial prejudice because he had not made changing his attitudes a priority. In our preaching and teaching all of us need to remember that some people still do not understand the significance of loving the neighbor as a part of true discipleship.

The pastor's wife was Korean. A large Asian population had moved into the community around the church. The church opened its doors so that a Korean congregation could worship in their sanctuary and use all of their facilities. The pastor's wife was in a women's meeting and was shocked to hear the women of the church talk about how they didn't like the way the church smelled after the Asians cooked in it. They began discussing whether or not "they" should continue to be allowed to use the church. Finally the pastor's wife had heard enough and said, "This conversation is hurting me. Don't you realize that I am Asian? I am one of 'them.' " One of the women said, "No you aren't. You are one of us!" It was certainly a painful incident, but the pastor's wife reminded the congregation that when we love and accept people, differences can disappear. She was being the bridge between communities that Jesus intends us all to be.

Cultural conflict can also be a problem in the small membership church. We like to think that America is a place where class is not an issue. Unfortunately, when a church is made up of a few families or the members are from the same neighborhood, everyone tends to be at a similar place on the socioeconomic scale. Regardless of where the church members see themselves socially, they are uncomfortable when someone comes in from what is perceived as a different class. This can occur when people arrive that the members think might be "uppity" and "look down on" them. Until they prove that they are "regular" people, they might not be treated with love and acceptance.

The same is true when someone arrives that the congregation perceives as "not good enough" to be accepted. This might include people with obvious addictions, people who are homeless, or those who are obviously mentally ill. Many years ago a church I pastored was also studying the Gospel of Luke. A central theme in the Gospel is that Jesus had a special place in his heart for the misfits, the unloved, and the outcasts. Each week I emphasized this theme. Several chapters into the Gospel a woman from a neighboring community who was considered by many to be obnoxious, dirty, and unprincipled, began to attend church and the Bible study. Soon after that, a person who was an obvious addict arrived. Was God sending these people to us as a test to see if we were getting the message that we should love *all* people?

FEAR

Many churches are just plain afraid. Anything that presents change for them may seem a real challenge. Someone taught me that the seven last words of the church are always: "We have never done it this way!" Individually and collectively many churches resist change. Fear is often related to loss of control. Fear sometimes arises when a congregation confronts anything new or different.

Fear expresses itself in many different ways. Once in a while a member will say to me, "David, I'm afraid that if we . . ." However, fear, like racial conflict, often becomes masked as something else. Sometimes it is masked as anger. Recently a neighboring church voted to begin an interracial ministry. The church was white and it was seeking to reach out to an African American church in the community. Suddenly anger toward the pastor began to surface. The issues raised were pretty complex, but underneath the presenting issues was a lot of fear on the part of the members.

Sometimes fear can come from relationships with other churches or with the denomination. The small membership church may feel that church administrators or boards are not hearing its voice. The close proximity of other churches may lead to fear. The congregation may fear that another church will proselyte and take its members away.

Beneath all this may be a fear that another church, especially a church with more resources is "better than we are." Other issues such as envy may cloud the issue.

Sometimes fears are well grounded in reality. A fairly large nondenominational church is located in our county. It is only a few miles from one of my churches. Several years ago Bonnie, one of our members, was experiencing some personal struggles. A friend from the larger church showed up at her house with her pastor. The friend told Bonnie she hoped she did not mind that she brought Pastor Goodfaith along, but hoped he would say prayers that would help. Bonnie felt very uncomfortable about this but did not know how to tell Pastor Goodfaith that she was uncomfortable. After praying, Pastor Goodfaith told Bonnie that if she became uncomfortable with her church she might want to try attending his church.

Painful as all the various kinds of conflict are, they are never the final stage of spiritual formation. Spiritual leadership does demand, however, that they be recognized and dealt with.

CHAPTER 5

Moving Beyond the Roadblocks

Pastor and the congregation share the leadership role necessary to move beyond the roadblocks. The pastor must not personalize the conflict. If this happens the pastor then becomes a part of the problem. In fact, the pastor can quickly become the problem.

Both the pastor and the small membership church must work together to move beyond conflict. They must all keep in mind the stages of spiritual growth. They must keep in mind the parable of the Garden. Together they must work for the kind of congregation whose deep, rich soil continually yields a harvest of fruit for the kingdom. How are they to move beyond the roadblocks?

THE ROLE OF PASTORAL CARE

The importance of the pastoral care ministry of the church cannot be overstated. Pastoral care is not necessarily pastoral counseling. Counseling is a rather narrowly defined form of pastoral care in which the caregiver acts as counselor or therapist to a church member or group of church members. There is often an identified problem to be addressed and worked on. Pastoral care, on the other hand, is a much broader practice. It may be defined

as the art of applying God's love to the members of a congregation, the community, and the world. It is a part of every ministry
of the church. Administration, worship, missions, and teaching
are all areas of ministry that are to be done within a ministry of
pastoral care. It has to do with the nurture of souls. If conflicts are
a sickness of the soul, then pastoral care is one of the greatest
tools the pastor and the church have in healing and resolving
conflict and overcoming roadblocks.

In 1971 I was finishing seminary by taking a quarter of Clinical
Pastoral Education (CPE). CPE is training in pastoral care and
counseling and is designed to help one learn to give pastoral care.
I was assigned to a nursing home and served as chaplain to the
residents and staff there.

At that point in my life I was young and unsure about the tal-
ents that God had given me for ministry. I just knew that I felt
and heard God's call, and that somehow God wanted me to minister to others. A very gruff private-duty nurse guarded one of my
patients. Every day when I called on Mr. Jones I was met by this
nurse who would answer my knock at the door with, "Yes, what
do you want?" I would tell her that I was the chaplain and that I
had come to see Mr. Jones. She would tell me that he was well
and that I could not see him, and then she would slam the door
in my face. I would not have continued to go back each week, but
I knew that my supervisor checked a visitation log that I kept,
and if I did not visit a particular patient, I would have to explain
why. Going to Mr. Jones's room and having the door slammed in
my face seemed to be easier than explaining.

Finally, one day the nurse answered the door, and as she was getting ready to slam it, Mr. Jones called out, "Who is it?" When the
nurse told him that I was the chaplain he said, "Tell him to come
in." I entered the room to find him sitting up in bed. He was smil-
ing and seemed very glad to see me. His wife was sitting beside the
bed. He told me to have a seat. I held out my hand, introduced
myself, and asked him how he was doing. He smiled and said, "Well,
I'm dying." I do not remember what I said after that. I just remember that he seemed to have a sense of peace within himself. He
went on to tell me a lot about the experience of living and dying.

Several days later Mr. Jones died. A week or so after his death I was in a supervisory session with my supervisor, Zeke. He asked me if I was aware that the Jones family had complained about my work. I was shocked, and I asked Zeke what I had done wrong. He told me to quit feeling sorry for myself. He said, "You did a great job. I don't know what you did, but my advice to you is to keep on doing it. He knew he was dying and he wanted to talk with someone. You gave him the chance. His family did not want to hear it, but he needed to say those things and have his family hear them. You were the catalyst that enabled it to happen. If you put yourself in situations so that God can use you, things like that happen."

Through the coming years I was to find that Zeke had been right. Woody Allen once said that 80 percent of success in life comes from just showing up. You could say that 80 percent of my success in ministry came out of just showing up. God does the rest. I can't tell you the number of times people have quoted things from sermons that I preached that gave them comfort or strength, only they were things I don't remember saying. They heard what God wanted them to hear. To my amazement I often ended up at the right place at the right time. Miraculously, some experience that I had coincided with what was happening with someone who needed to know that they were not alone. I will tell you that a large part of the other 20 percent of my ministry that went right was loving other people. I found that if I did show up, and if I loved and cared about the people I was with, that God did do the rest.

It is important to note that loving people may not be the same as liking or enjoying them. Love is not so much a feeling as it is an attitude or way of relating. When John writes that "God so loved the world" he is not talking about God necessarily enjoying or liking all that the human race is involved in. Rather, John is saying that the very being of God radiates a quality of attitude and relationship that puts the well-being of the world above any self-interest that God may have.

Like most things in the life of the church, pastoral care is a shared responsibility. The people have a responsibility to love the pastor, each other, the community, and the world. It is the job of the pastor to teach members that the things they do in their everyday life and work can provide pastoral care to the community. In loving people we identify and encourage their gifts.

A member of one of my small churches had visions and they seemed to be related to the diagnosis and healing of physical illness. Through prayer and spiritual direction I began encouraging her to explore and use her gifts. Today she has a newsletter and prayer ministry that has an impact on hundreds of people across several states. A member of a small membership church began to ask others if he could sponsor them on a Walk to Emmaus. As of this writing there are more than twenty-five people that he and his wife have now sponsored. About ten of them are from his congregation. This initiative by one person has done remarkable things to renew this congregation. This one servant uses Emmaus to help encourage the gifts of others.

Every church is filled with examples of how members provide pastoral care to one another. When the pastor demonstrates an attitude of love and acceptance toward the members, they feel more comfortable showing love and acceptance toward one another.

MOVING BEYOND THE ROADBLOCKS BY SETTING THE ENVIRONMENT

Consider ways that the love and nurture of God is demonstrated through the life and work of the church. This begins with things that are as simple as accessibility. Are handicapped parking spaces made available close to the church? Are there ramps for wheelchairs and people with walkers? Are aisles wide enough to accommodate wheelchairs? Is there an elevator? Do the acoustics or sound system enable hearing-impaired members to hear the service? If not, is signing available? Is there a nursery provided for families with small children?

If these things are available, do you advertise them? How do you advertise? Word of mouth by the members to nonmembers is highly effective. It reaches people with special needs as an act of hospitality on the part of the membership. If a person in the community realizes that the congregation cares enough about them to provide for their special needs, they are likely to feel loved and welcomed.

Consider ways that the administrative structure of the church supports the pastoral care ministry of the congregation. Early in my years in ministry I began a practice of having people who are in conflict with each other work together. At a Harvest Sale, for example, I often put people who did not like each other at tables to work together. Working side by side on a common project that needs little leadership but instead focuses on a simple task can help people see that they can get along. Do the administrative structures of your church allow people with differences to work together to solve simple shared problems? Is an effort made to include people with special needs among the leadership of the church? Are meetings as accessible as worship?

MOVING BEYOND THE ROADBLOCKS THROUGH THE USE OF SYMBOLS

Many years ago I attended a small membership Presbyterian Church. The sanctuary walls were mostly glass. The windows looked out onto a garden. They also looked out onto the parking lot beside the church and the highway in front of the church. The view that focused on the garden was beautiful and inspirational. The other views were sometimes beautiful and sometimes not very pleasant. The overall effect, however, was to remind us that our mission was beyond our walls. Whenever the congregation assembled to worship they always had their eyes turned toward the community and world they were called to serve.

Churches communicate and teach many things through the symbols they use. Many contemporary churches seem to be built with few windows. Other churches seem to be built with stained glass windows that honor the saints of their past. A pastor and congregation should be familiar with their church building. They need to ask themselves what the building is saying symbolically. Two of the churches on the Burkeville Charge have rather large cemeteries beside them. Frequently I mention the saints of the past and talk about how they are still united with us. The important thing is to integrate the congregation's life with the building and surroundings.

In our churches we have begun using lighted candles at board meetings and Bible study. I frequently mention that the candles remind us of the presence of God. They focus our attention on the presence and bring us together when tensions arise.

MOVING BEYOND THE ROADBLOCKS THROUGH MEANS OF GRACE

The act of Holy Communion is of the greatest importance in overcoming spiritual roadblocks. In Holy Communion we *come together* at the altar. The unity found in the taking of Holy Communion has many dimensions, but the key one is that if each of us is united with Christ, then each of us is also united with each other. We are united not only with those in our own time and space, but with all of those who have participated in the meal in the past, all who participate in the present, and those who will participate in the future. This helps us see ourselves a part of a larger plan in which our petty conflicts mean little. The ritual brings all people to the altar so that we can become living sacrifices for Jesus in return for God's sacrifice for us through him. It calls us to be one with the world that suffers.

Earlier I mentioned women from a small membership church who take Holy Communion to a shelter for battered women. The way that Holy Communion is able to bring healing is in itself a remarkable study. One Sunday morning I celebrated Holy Communion for the first time with a church where I had just been appointed. The text that Sunday was on Zacchaeus. I talked about how he did not allow being short to keep him from seeing

Jesus. As the service ended with Holy Communion one woman whose hands were severely twisted with rheumatoid arthritis came forward to receive the sacrament. The woman's daughter later told me that the former pastor had refrained from shaking hands with her mother for fear that he would hurt her. She had been so embarrassed by what she interpreted as rejection that she had stopped taking communion. The Sunday morning I preached on Zacchaeus she had decided not to let her handicap keep her from being close to Jesus. The sacrament has the power to heal and transform. It is our responsibility as spiritual leaders to make it as available as possible. This means bringing the elements to the seats of those who wish to participate but cannot walk down to receive it. This means taking Holy Communion to members who are homebound and members in nursing homes on a regular basis. Many churches are now having teams of members volunteer to do this.

Prayer is vital for overcoming roadblocks. In a period of prayer concerns, is there mention of the things that divide members? There are almost fifty pastoral appointments in our district. One of our churches prays for another of the pastoral appointments every week. Every member of the congregation does that. It is a discipline that focuses their spiritual thoughts and energies beyond themselves. Do we pray for our enemies? Too often churches focus only on those of us who are members or those of us who are friends and allies. Remember that Jesus says we must pray for our enemies and bless those who persecute us. Recently one of our members told me that at first she found it odd that I would ask us to pray for our enemies. Perhaps pastors do not spend enough time asking members to pray for those who are a threat or danger to us.

From time to time in Bible study and worship I mention the placement of the altar and cross in the sanctuary. Whenever the congregation gathers it faces the altar and cross. When an offering is taken it is placed on the altar. A congregation knows these things at one level, but consciously teaching them is important. It helps integrate their understanding of acts of worship with their understanding of the space in which they worship.

CHAPTER 6

Arriving at Inclusion

M oses and the Israelites wandered around the desert for forty years. Spiritual growth is always a journey. The pastor or the congregation must understand that the journey may be long and dangerous. It may be tedious. It may also be exciting and fulfilling.

The early church quickly came to understand that the goal of the journey toward spiritual maturity is inclusion. When the church first received the Holy Spirit as recorded in Acts 2 there were people present from every part of the known world. Quickly the Acts narrative tells us of the church's growing understanding of the gospel's application to all people. An angel sends Philip to an Ethiopian eunuch in Acts 8; Saul—Paul—is named as the one who is to be the instrument for bringing the gospel to the Gentiles in Acts 9; Peter has a vision in which he learns that it is not right to consider unclean what God has blessed and considers clean in Acts 10. The New Testament ends with the vision of the New Jerusalem found in Revelation 21–22. The final vision is universal in scope. It says that people will come into this holy city from all nations. Indeed, the vision ends with the image of the tree of life. Its fruit will bring healing to the nations.

The New Testament thus ends with the same thrust toward which the worship service is patterned. The Bible itself ends with the call to welcome all and show hospitality to all. As mentioned above, the journey is long. There are several attitudes that are helpful to the small membership congregation. These are considered below along with several strategies for programming.

ATTITUDES OF INCLUSION AND HOSPITALITY

Earlier we considered the spiritual practices. We saw how they pull the individual and the congregation into a deeper relationship with God. This deeper relationship brings a deeper awareness of God's presence in our lives, community, and world. What we practice is what we do. It shapes us into what we are. What we are begins to become apparent in the spiritual stages of integrity and inclusion. As these attitudes develop they lead us into deeper engagement with God's world. Attitudes have much to do with shaping our behavior.

Gratitude

One of the most important attitudes to encourage in yourself and your congregation is *gratitude*. Gratitude is a feeling of appreciation and thankfulness. We feel appreciation and thankfulness when we receive a gift. Gratitude is our response to the gift of God's love.

As the spiritual leader, you can only find gratitude in your life as minister if you are truly grateful to God for the small membership church you serve. You must be able to bless and be grateful for this particular time and place in your life. When you look at your ministry and your appointment you may sometimes wonder what you have to be grateful for. Many of us spend a lot of time and energy looking at pastors with larger churches and larger salaries. If we are honest with ourselves about the way our lives and work are unfolding in light of the way we envision ourselves and our ministry, we might want to ask something like: "Is this the way call to ministry winds up?" Fortunately, gratitude has a way of changing the way we see situations and events in our lives.

Gratitude also has a way of changing the way we see others. To be truly grateful is to appreciate all that other people do for us each day. The truth is that we are all so connected to God and to each other that to experience gratitude is to feel in harmony with everyone and everything in creation. To feel gratitude is to realize that we are not alone. We are loved. Perhaps you feel that you and your congregation are not capable of this type of gratitude. Begin where you are. Lead your people in counting their blessings as a faith community. You will all find that your feelings of gratitude will grow, and that they will begin to produce the fruits of which Jesus spoke in the parable of the Sower.

Earlier, when we looked at worship we considered how worship always begins with praise. Praise implies gratitude toward God. In fact, in the church we often speak of praise and thanksgiving together. Many of my prayers during worship emphasize the things for which we are thankful. Many years ago during a revival I prayed a long prayer in which I mentioned all the small things in life we are thankful for. I mentioned birds, trees, butterflies, the rain, our pets; the list went on and on for many minutes longer than my usual prayers. After the prayer one of my members, a cantankerous old woman who was a thorn in the flesh of many of the parishioners because of her anger and outspokenness, was crying. She cried quietly during the remainder of the service. Afterward she told me how much the prayer had meant to her—the first positive thing she had ever said to me. For a few minutes the angry woman had begun to feel grateful. It was a beginning.

In order to foster a feeling of gratitude in your congregation you must let them know that you appreciate and are thankful for them as individuals. I love to write and I write a lot of thank-you notes to my members. A member recently told my wife, "I get a thank-you note from David every time I turn around." I even write thank-you notes to the little ones who give me "refrigerator art" on Sunday morning. Maybe I sometimes carry the note writing to extremes. When I learned that a six-year-old boy in the congregation had gotten his ear pierced and on the way home had told his mother that he couldn't wait until Sunday so he could show his new earring to David, I wrote a note telling him how nice his new earring looked on Sunday and thanking him for showing it to me. Note writing keeps me in the habit of seeing all kinds of experiences as gifts from the people I serve, and letting them know that I'm grateful.

It is also important to let your congregation know that you appreciate and are thankful for them as the body of Christ. In our church we periodically have appreciation Sundays. Sunday school teachers, our women's group and our men's group all have times when they are recognized for their service. We could easily carry the concept further and have recognition Sundays for every committee and organization within the church. Everyone feels more loved and appreciated when we let them know that we are grateful for the things that they do. When the church gathers for the ninetieth birthday of a faithful member, we are uniting to show our gratitude. When we celebrate the fiftieth anniversary of a couple who have worked tirelessly for the Lord we, as the body of Christ, are showing our gratitude.

The concept of *gratitude* is so important that it is a cornerstone of physical and mental health. People in recovery from addictions are sometimes taught to establish an *attitude of gratitude*. This is more than simply having a positive attitude; it involves beginning to see *everything* that happens in the light of God's love and grace. Even in suffering we learn to find opportunities for growth. A dear lady spent years visiting and writing to people on behalf of a prestigious university, trying to find out how heredity in her family and other families in the community influenced rheumatoid arthritis, the disease that caused her to use a wheelchair from a young age. An African American church in our area used their experience of suffering to reach out to the Latino children of migrant workers in an after-school program.

Gratitude has a way of increasing as we begin to reflect on our blessings. It grows and so fills our spirits that there is decreasing room for bitterness and anger. To be truly grateful is to have little room for self-pity or envy. To have a spirit of gratitude within our heart is to have no room for the petty frustrations we often feel toward others. To have a spirit of gratitude invites the community to share openly without fear. If we are people of gratitude we are likely to be a happy community who enjoys being who we are and looks forward to being who we are called to be.

Humility

Consider another attitude—humility. Moving from gratitude to humility is not easy for some people or communities. This is not an attitude that comes easily in our culture. Much in our culture stresses pride. From childhood we learn about things like national pride, ethnic pride, and all of us know the joy that comes from having a parent say "I'm proud of you!" We are proud of our church or denomination. We want our congregation to have a sense of pride in the things it does. Not all pride is bad.

There are times, however, when pride inhibits our spiritual growth. In fact, pride can be destructive. The church considers pride to be one of the seven deadly sins. The pride that the church is concerned about is the pride that keeps us from acknowledging our dependence on God. This type of pride can be called *hubris*. It is a failure to humble ourselves before God. The best models for his type of pride in the Bible are Adam and Eve. Their real sin is in failing to be obedient to God. You know the story. God puts them in creation where they can live and enjoy the bounty around them. The only prohibition is eating the fruit from one particular tree. Adam and Eve decide to break the prohibition and set their own rules. To paraphrase the song sung by Frank Sinatra, "They did it *their* way."

In our culture we place a high value on self-determinism. We tend to honor the self-made man. Indeed, we often honor the independent church that seems to be led by a self-made pastor. The danger is that we, as individuals or communities of faith, will fail to honor and respect the limits that God puts on us.

Humility, on the other hand, is acknowledgment of our limits. Humility is simply accepting ourselves as we are—finite, limited creatures created and loved by a loving and limitless God. It means that we acknowledge that our relationship with God is not a private thing. God has created us to be a family. Jesus made this clear in his teachings. In Romans 8:15-17 Paul spoke of becoming God's child as being a matter of adoption into God's family. Being part of a family means that we have a moral obligation to each other and to God. We do not have the right to make up our own rules in life. We do not have the right to set our own destiny. Christianity teaches that we are not our own people. We were bought at a price—the price of Jesus' sacrifice. Through this sacrifice we are brought into God's family and have a special obligation to others and the world. The concept that best describes this obligation is *stewardship*. That has to do with trust and responsibility rather than ownership. In truth none of us owns anything. All is of God and all belongs to God. We are simply servants of God who are entrusted with taking care of or developing what ultimately belongs to God.

Pride leads us to claim and attempt to take. Humility, on the other hand, leads us to give. It literally opens the door to hospitality and inclusion. Rather than being concerned about receiving *what is coming to us*, humility brings concern over how we can best *serve*. The pastor should always be an example of humility to the congregation. One loving and humble pastor was the United States Army Chief of Chaplains. This made him a two-star general. During the Vietnam War he made a visit there. All of the Army chaplains serving were invited to attend a luncheon with him. He quietly left his seat, picked up a pitcher of water and went from table to table serving the guests. The leader became the humble servant.

We only have to look closely at Jesus to begin to understand humility. He was born in a stable, worked as a carpenter. He willingly washed the feet of his friends. He willingly gave up his life for his friends and for all of us. Perhaps the most beautiful passage in the entire New Testament is the Philippian hymn found in Paul's Letter to the Philippians 2:5-11. Paul writes that we should have the same mind as Christ who humbled himself. It is worth reading often.

I once knew a wonderful pastor who had a picture of Pinocchio on his desk. You know who Pinocchio was. He was a puppet on strings. He moved when someone pulled the strings. This pastor was always complaining that people were pulling his strings. Most of us are uncomfortable when we feel that someone is pulling our strings or causing us to react. We would rather be in control of our own lives. We would rather set our own goals and move toward them. The pastor told me that one of the women in his parish gave him the picture to remind him that when someone pulled his strings he was doing ministry. That is a powerful insight. Perhaps it is when others pull our strings that we all do ministry.

When we let God pull our strings we are led to places more wonderful than we could have imagined. When we respond to the needs of our church members we are being the faithful servant God wants us to be. When we teach our parish that we must respond to the needs of the community and the world we are helping them to become more Christlike. Taking a group of young people to a local homeless shelter to help serve Thanksgiving dinner is teaching them what it means to serve. Having the preschoolers in the church make cards for members who are homebound is teaching them to be Christians. Encouraging the women's group to go to the home of a member of the community who has a disability and clean her house and yard is encouraging them to show love and compassion to those less fortunate. Reach outside your church to people of different racial and ethnic groups. Serve *all* the people within your reach.

Humility heightens our experience of the presence of God. Like all the practices we have considered, and like the attitude of gratitude, humility does not come easily or quickly. Begin where you and your parish are at this moment. Let the things you think about, the work you do, and prayers you offer to God lead you.

Acceptance

He is a runner. He looks like a runner. He is tall and thin. He is also on crutches. Several weeks ago he broke his ankle. He begins to tell me about plans to run in the Boston Marathon next year. He talks about being disappointed that he will have to remain in the hospital another day. "I'm not used to being still," he tells me. Suddenly he shrugs and says, "I'm disappointed that I'm not going to be released today, but it must be that God has another mission for me here." He smiles as he begins the walk back to his room. I like this young man very much. He is teaching me a lesson about spirituality. Sometimes we need to accept the fact that God is in charge.

The Bible begins with the story of creation. One of the very clear messages of this story is that God's original intent for humanity was perfect life lived in paradise. While God may have initially intended for us to live in paradise, it is our lot to live our lives in a land *east of Eden* where struggle and suffering are realities of human experience. Surely the realities of your small membership church bring you to such a place.

All of us have a longing for paradise, and all of us have a sense of how life should be. Life is not always easy or fair. How do we, then, live in a world that often hurts or threatens to destroy us or the ones we love without being bitter or afraid? How do we experience the presence of God when we live separated from God? How do we experience the holy and lead others to experience the holy in a world that is often broken and is certainly not paradise? How does the body of Christ gather to praise God on the Sunday following the tragic death of a church member on Saturday night?

Perhaps the way to begin is to have an attitude of acceptance. Acceptance is simply living with the reality of what is. Acceptance becomes easier when we begin to realize that it is in a broken world of thorns and stones that we experience God. Reading or praying the Psalms can help. The benefits of using Psalms in your private devotions, and of beginning every worship service with a reading of the Psalms were discussed earlier. The Psalms are often prayers of praise and they are often written within the context of suffering or brokenness. Jesus, for example, quoted Psalm 22, while he suffered on the cross. "My God, my God, why have you forsaken me?" is anything but a word of denial. It is an anguished cry of acceptance of a suffering that is so dark that it blocks out the experience of the divine presence.

If you read this psalm, however, you will find that acceptance does not mean surrender to the darkness. The psalm ends in words of praise. The psalmist knows that it is possible to find faith and healing by openly acknowledging and accepting the realities of life. Other psalms echo this same theme. The ancient Israelites were aware that God was found in the darkness.

This theme is reflected throughout the Bible. It finds its highest point in the suffering of Jesus on the cross. As stated above Jesus accepted his suffering and even quoted Psalm 22 from the cross. Paul reflected on suffering and wrote the beautiful words of Romans 8—that the sufferings of this age are not worth comparing with the glory that awaits us, and that no amount or degree of suffering can separate us from the love of God in Jesus Christ. You see, faith gives us a context in which to accept suffering and move from the darkness into light.

Having the courage to look into the darkness is not easy. It often takes lots of practice of the spiritual disciplines mentioned earlier—worship, Bible study, receiving Holy Communion, lots of prayer, and spiritual friendships. As our thoughts and spirits become shaped and focused toward the presence of God in our lives and in the life of the congregation the easier it is to look into the darkness. The more our spirits are shaped by the presence of God the easier it becomes to reach out to others in the darkness.

One of the greatest lessons taught me in this life came from one of our former family pastors. I bumped into him one morning at a time when I was worried about a lot of things that seemed to be going wrong in my life. When I asked him how he was doing he answered, "Canada, it's been rough. Last year my wife died. Then I was forced to retire because I turned seventy. Then I had to enter a retirement home. But through it all I have learned one thing. The most difficult task any of us has is to accept the reality of our lives." That may be the most profound thing anyone has ever said to me. Those words still inspire and challenge me. Ultimately, I may not be able to change some of the important things in my life or in the life of my parish. It may be that I simply have to accept them as they are.

Earlier I mentioned another person who had a profound impact upon my life, Carlyle Marney. He always had a beautiful way of seeing and expressing things. He used to teach clergy that they could never bless other people until they learn how to bless themselves. The same can be said of congregations no matter how small or large. Blessing myself means accepting my life as it is and receiving it from God with gratitude rather than bitterly complaining about how cursed I am. Marney reminded me that we do not have a choice as to whether or not we suffer. Our choice is, rather, whether our suffering is unto *death* or unto *life*. To suffer unto life is to be able to accept the reality of the suffering and brokenness in our own lives and in the life of our community of faith, and to find God in the midst of what appears to be darkness.

Many of us have trouble accepting the reality of our lives because of some mistake or mistakes we have made. Congregations have the same problem. We may have to live with the consequences of poor decisions. It may be that our decisions have hurt others. It may be hard for us to forgive ourselves. I have friends who are always in spiritual turmoil because they feel they *should* have been better people during their younger years. Regrets often stand in the way of our acceptance of our lives. Sometimes acceptance becomes more difficult as we get older and are faced with problems that are the result of decisions made many years ago. I believe the answer to this particular dilemma is to be found in focusing not on our past mistakes, but rather on God's unconditional love for us. If we can begin to see ourselves as God sees us we will better accept the reality of our individual lives and of our shared life together as a small community of God. If we can begin to understand the unconditional grace of God we will begin to feel the love that God truly has for each of us. If we can begin to "accept our own acceptance," as one famous theologian wrote, we will begin to more fully experience the presence of God in the midst of the darkness we perceive in our lives, our church, and our world. I believe that God does not have as much trouble forgiving us as we have forgiving ourselves and accepting God's forgiveness. God does not have

the same trouble accepting the reality of our lives that we continually have.

As with the practices and attitudes mentioned previously, the
key to acceptance is found in beginning where you are. If you and
your congregation will take your concerns to God and ask for
divine help in accepting yourselves and your shared life, God will
help. Healing will begin. The presence of God will become a
more conscious part of your life. The divine light will begin to
illuminate the dark corners. Others who walk in darkness will be
attracted to the light they see.

With acceptance comes a letting go of hurt and bitterness.
With acceptance comes a new way of seeing things, a new way of
living relationships, a freedom to forgive and to be forgiven.

Detachment

If there are things in our lives that cannot be changed and that
simply must be accepted, what are we to do? When all around us
we are confronted by people who are angry, lost, overwhelmed,
and hurt, how do we survive the pain? When the world thrusts an
endless stream of information at us through the media, what are
we to think? One attitude that can help us is that of detachment.
Detachment releases the mind to reach out to God and discern
God's will in the midst of confusion.

Detachment, however, is a concept that many of us have trouble understanding. For years I thought it had to do with not being
involved or not caring. I identified people as being detached if
they seemed not to care about me or other people. A friend
helped me reconsider detachment when he told me that Jesus
had a kind of detachment. At first I had trouble understanding
that, because one thing I knew about Jesus was that he was com-
passionate. How could someone with enough compassion to die
for the sins of the world also be detached?

Consider Jesus' actions. He did cure the sick and raise the
dead. He also, in miraculous ways, fed hungry people. He touched
people who were considered unclean. At the same time he was

able to get away by himself to pray. He was able to take care of those whose needs seemed the most pressing but was also able to live with a sense of peace and serenity while he took seriously the failings of others and the brokenness of the world.

When we become detached we do not detach ourselves from the people and events in our lives and in our world. We detach ourselves from our own egos so we can see those people and events with clarity. Detachment, like acceptance, is built on a foundation of faith and understanding that encourages us to see things as God sees them. When we detach we are removing ourselves from the things that separate us from God—pride, anger, envy, fear—the roadblocks our egos put between us and God.

Many of us go through life carrying resentment for things others have done to us. Anger takes a lot of time and energy. I am guilty of this but I also must admit that it seems that most of the people who have hurt me in life were not trying to hurt me at all. I just happened to be in their way. Whatever happened to me was usually a result of someone else thinking I was a threat to them or somehow stood in the way of their own security or fulfillment. Seeing others and seeing circumstances in this way helps me let go of resentment and anger. Detachment means letting go of anger and frustration that consumes time and energy.

Lately we often hear people say, "Let go and let God." "Letting go and letting God" is detachment. It is trusting to God those things that are beyond our reach or control. Rather than lack of care or compassion, detachment reflects the highest form of love. It reflects the attitude Jesus demonstrated. It means having enough love and concern to take the problem to God. It means trusting in the goodness and love of God enough to trust God to care more than we do and have more power than we do to solve the problem. It reminds us that God loves the church far more than we can. It calls to mind the fact that all of creation is in God's hand and that God wills healing and wholeness—salvation—for all. God wills inclusion and hospitality.

Our egos have often kept us, individually and collectively, from experiencing God's presence. Think of all the problems in your own life that have been caused because of a bruised ego.

Look back on the history of your congregation. Think of the divisions in the church, the hurt feelings, the number of people who have left the church because of an unkind word or what was perceived as an unkind word. How often have you become defensive when criticized? How often have your committee meetings ended in anger or resentment? The ego is a fragile thing and responsible for so many divisions. How many of your parishioners see a neighbor as the enemy?

It is only when we detach from the real enemy, our ego, that an alignment with God is possible. Detachment frees us from the old ways we have seen people, places, and things. It enables us to let go of our emotional baggage: old hurts, old prejudices, and old worries. In so freeing our spirits it opens them to the possibility that they will have enough space to hold the good things God intends for us. In allowing us to release the old ways we have viewed the church and all who are in it, detachment allows us to have the eyes of Jesus. These are the eyes of true compassion. They are able to view the world and to view others without the burdens of hurt feelings, bruised egos, or broken dreams. Detachment frees us to experience each moment as children who are alive to the joy and wonder and possibility of what God may be creating and revealing to us.

One church was so small that a man held several key leadership positions. As he grew older his influence and the number of his positions grew. He began to speak of the church as "my church." His wife did the same. At first the church did not notice. Over time changes happened in his life and he became angry and resentful over issues in his life, his family, and his community. The feelings of anger and resentment spread to his feelings toward the church. He became angry when new members had new ideas. One very perceptive district superintendent told the pastor he believed that this member was "holding the church hostage." The pastor began a simple strategy of saying in sermons, newsletters, and meetings, "It is not your church nor my church. It is God's church." The pastor began to raise this issue in board meetings and asked for prayers before votes or in the middle of arguments. The prayers called for detachment—a letting go and turning the issue over to God. Over a period of several months things began to change—even the angry man's attitude. The church was letting go of self-interest and moving toward God's interest.

God has given us a powerful capacity to deal with pressures. It is the capacity to trust and thus detach. What is most important is that the one whom we trust is the one who is the source of all trust. The one who is the source is the one who is love—pure love—God.

Anticipation

Another attitude that comes from inclusion is anticipation. Kathy taught me a lesson about this long ago. We met shortly before her mother's death when Kathy was thirteen. On a Saturday before Easter several years later I was at church doing some things when Kathy arrived to visit her mother's grave. I went with her to the graveyard and we sat down on the grass and talked about a lot of things. Suddenly she smiled and said, "You know, Dave, I feel like something good is going to happen!"

She had just touched on one of the secrets of experiencing the presence of God and on one of the fruits of integrity and inclusion. The secret is to anticipate something good happening. It is to expect God to be present in a beautiful way. What was remarkable, as I look back on that day, is that Kathy was able to express that hope beside the grave of her mother. You see, God visits us in the darkest and most painful of places. To truly know hope as a Christian or as a community of faith is to be able to face the most painful of human situations—even the grave—with the awareness that something good is about to happen.

In the parable of the Sower Jesus talks about how God is always sowing seed. These seed are the divine presence, and God plants them in our lives. This activity is intended to create in all of us an awareness of God's presence. It is God's intention that we experience this presence in the activities of our daily lives. We may think of the presence as something we only feel on Sundays when we are in church or we may think of it as something available to us only in prayer and meditation. It is, however, always there and can become real to us at any time and in any event.

My friend Kathy understood that one of the key ways in which we prepare ourselves for the experience is to anticipate it in hope. The more we look for it the more likely we are to see and recognize it. Perhaps if we are not experiencing the presence of God as we would like to we need to ask ourselves if we are really looking for it.

For many years I have begun almost every sermon by reading one of the comics from that day's Sunday paper. It is so anticipated by the congregation that many people begin to laugh when I say, "How many of you read today's comics?" It's amazing that there is *always* at least one comic that has a direct relationship with the day's sermon. My favorites are *Peanuts*, *The Family Circus*, *Blondie*, *Shoe*, and *Beetle Bailey*; but there are often others I use. The purpose of this weekly exercise is not just to entertain and amuse. It is a conscious decision to demonstrate that God's word can be found in every aspect of our lives if we just look for it. It is important for your congregation to know that God is still active in the world today. That God is still imparting wisdom and that it is our responsibility as Christians to look for it. God is still giving us answers to the moral dilemmas that we face in the modern world.

Perhaps you have had the following experience while driving down a road you have traveled many times. If you are hungry you may start looking for a restaurant. You may realize that you have never seen a restaurant on that road before, but suddenly you may see one in front of you. It may be that you have passed that particular restaurant many times and never seen it because you were not hungry and were not looking for it. One problem all people have these days is that we are bombarded by more information than we need. Whenever we turn on a radio or television or open our mailbox or walk down the street we hear or see advertisements or information we do not need. Our senses are so bombarded that we have all learned to tune out those things we do not need to be aware of. If we need the information we search for it. Our senses become heightened in our search if we really need that for which we look.

The same is true of God's presence. It is in the world all around us, but you and I may have been so conditioned to look for other things that we may not see the need or value of seeking it. If our religious faith is only something that prepares for an afterlife we may not think of the need to experience the divine presence in our daily journey. If, on the other hand, we think of the divine presence as something that we need and that we are able to find on the road of our daily lives, we are far more likely to be prepared for finding it and thus are far more likely to do so.

Whenever someone comes to me with a concern about their life I always ask if they know where God is in the concern. It makes no difference what the concern is. It may be an illness, it may be an upcoming wedding, it may be selecting the right school to attend, it may involve difficulty in getting along with a spouse or parent. Frequently people are able to identify an awareness of God's presence in the midst of the problem. Frequently people seem to have no idea that God is actually involved in the situation, and that it is possible to experience the living divine presence in the midst of the problem.

The difference is often anticipation. It is believing that God may indeed be revealed to us in the next moment. It is believing that God may become real to us in the next turn of events. It is the deep belief that God will be seen in the evangelism program the church is undertaking.

Anticipation depends upon our trust in God. The most commonly used word to describe God's nature in the Old Testament is *hesed*. It means *steadfast love*. The concept means that though times change and people change God's loving involvement in our lives remains constant. Experiencing the presence of God in our lives often depends upon our trusting that God is love and that God is involved in our lives, and then consciously anticipating that we will find God as we journey.

Assurance

Assurance goes a bit beyond the attitudes mentioned above. It can be described as a point at which doubts somehow are put aside and the individual, or congregation, is able to move forward without reservation. It is a state of knowing that we know. Some churches have reached a point of maturity that allows them to make decisions by consensus. This is really possible only through a process of discernment. A congregation discusses and seeks to discern the will of God. In such a system there is generally neither debating nor voting. There is prayer, discussion, and there is decision. The entire process is aimed not at trying to do what the majority of the people want, but by attempting to discern the will of God. This depth of discernment allows the congregation then to move on, knowing that they have turned the matter over to God. Even this may not give the people an experience of assurance. However, I am convinced that an intentional process of discernment is the best way to reach this state.

Sometimes assurance is not possible until we look back at a completed program or action. The Burkeville Charge's three churches were originally four churches. About a decade ago one of the churches, Barker Memorial, had reached a point at which they no longer felt that they were a viable congregation. Most of the older members had died and most of the younger members had grown up and moved away. Only a few members remained in the church. Just raising a minimal budget that allowed the congregation to pay its bills became a burden. One of the other churches on the charge, Ward's Chapel, invited Barker Memorial to join them. The process was long and involved. It began with prayer and struggle. It continued with discussion. After much anguish on the part of all of the members of Barker Memorial and some of the members of Ward's Chapel the decision was made to merge the congregations. Some of the furnishings from the Barker Memorial sanctuary were brought to Ward's Chapel. One of the rooms was named the "Barker Memorial Chapel." A plaque was put over the door that designated the room as such. Inside the room the altar, pulpit, and some of the pews were set up. The altar was set up for worship with the cross and other objects that had been set on it at Barker's. The Holy Communion set is also in that room. Beyond furnishings, specific action was taken to make some of the Barker members officers at Ward's. All but one of the members from Barker transferred their membership to Ward's. Now the two congregations have been truly formed into one. Recently one of the Barker members told me that she had struggled over the merger for years, and that it was only now after a decade that she knows she did the right thing. Even with the best strategies, it may be difficult to have a feeling of assurance.

Attributes

Images of restoration and renewal are found throughout the Bible and the history of the church. Stories of renewal are shared whenever Christians gather. In the parable of the Sower Jesus teaches us that the word or presence of God in our lives is like seeds that grow to mature plants and bear fruit. Sowing seed is something that must be done again every spring if there is to be a garden in the summer and a harvest in the fall. This annual act of planting seed is an example of renewal or restoration. For new crops to grow there must be a new planting of seed.

Too often we fail to remember that our spiritual journey must always be a thing of renewal or restoration. In a lot of churches *backsliding* is a familiar term. It usually refers to lapses in Christian faith or practice. Someone who has become an inactive church member is said to be a *backslider*. It may refer to someone who has made a bad moral choice. Sometimes the term is used to refer to people who have bad habits involving abuse of alcohol or drugs. The problem is that active Christians tend to look down on backsliders. Too often those of us in the church forget that it is only by God's steadfast love and grace that we ourselves have been restored or renewed.

Renewal is an action on God's part. It is the process of granting forgiveness to those who make mistakes. They may be individuals or communities. We often think of sin as an individual thing but it may also be a community thing. The struggles between God and the fallen nation of Israel are seen throughout the Psalms and Old Testament. The message of our faith is that God loves us individually and communally so much that there is always forgiveness and restoration available for the asking.

Renewal is not so much action on our part as it is a matter of asking and consciously opening ourselves to the tuning and revitalization that only God can give. It is not a matter of will or good works on our part. It is simply a matter of seeking and anticipating.

How is one or how is a community to ask for this restoration? There are resources to be found in the Bible and in our worship together as a community. Earlier the time of confession was discussed. In worship confession is both individual and communal. After confession there is a word of pardon and absolution.

Some of the most beautiful resources for restoration and renewal are found in Scriptures. The book of Psalms especially, contains beautiful and profound promises of renewal. Seven of the psalms are known as the penitential psalms. Since the fourth century they have been so categorized by the church. These are Psalms 6, 32, 38, 51, 102, 130, and 143. Take time this week to read over these psalms. Pray them. Encourage your church to read and pray them. They point the community back toward God and God restores the community. They point us back toward God as the one who sows the seed every spring. It must also be remembered that for the Christian it is always springtime and it is always Easter. God is always sowing and renewing.

STRATEGIES FOR INCLUSION AND HOSPITALITY

Ultimately a mature spiritual life is expressed in faith, hope, and love. Paul lists these attributes in 1 Corinthians 13:13. To some degree they are always there in the life of the believer.

They have been discussed through this book. I remember a church that had a large mural that covered an entire wall. Across it in bold colors was written: "Live Faith! Shout Hope! Love One Another!" I like that a lot. It could well be the theme of all of our small membership churches. As we integrate all of our spiritual experiences and learnings and begin to reach out, we do indeed live our faith, loudly proclaim our hope, and love one another. Consider again the parable. Consider strategies for moving toward inclusions as sowing seeds of faith, hope, and love.

Sowing Faith

Some years ago, while I was an Army chaplain stationed in Germany, I worked for a wonderful commander. Everyone loved working for Colonel Bill Jones. Everyone seemed to blossom under his leadership. He had a lot of confidence in our abilities, and usually gave us the freedom to carry out our mission as our training, experience, and judgment dictated. You would present an idea to Colonel Jones, and he would nod and say, "Make it happen!" I used to often shake my head in disbelief as things happened. The unit always seemed to work well, and on a given day it seemed that anyone was able to do the impossible. All it seemed to take was just showing up and a "Make it happen!" by someone who had faith in us.

Encouraging our church members to make things happen in their own lives and to give support to others in the congregation is important. However, there is a deeper dimension to the word *faith*. One of my favorite writings on faith is found in Hebrews 11. The chapter begins with a definition: "Now faith is the assurance of things hoped for, the conviction of things not seen." It has to do with belief in the future. Small membership churches often have a difficult time seeing into the future and appreciating things that they cannot see. If a church only has several active members it may have a hard time visioning a great future for itself.

Any strategy that sows seeds of faith—belief in what is in the future and thus unseen—should begin by acknowledging that there will be a future. I recently visited a church with a very small congregation and noticed that almost all of the objects in the sanctuary—from hymnals, to pictures, to furniture, to the piano—had a dedication plaque on it. Every object in the church was dedicated to the past. There was nothing in the room dedicated to the future!

One small membership church in our area had an architect draw up plans for renovations that will not take place for at least five years. The plans reflect the way that the congregation sees the needs of the church in the future. In designing the plans they were forced to plan ahead, to dream, and were inspired to change the way they do things to reflect their wishes for the future. These plans included the reality that an elevator will be needed for aging members. They also include a prayer garden to address the spiritual maturity that they plan to encourage in all members. Congregations grow older at the same time congregations are alive and growing. The congregation and the architect's plans will reflect the needs of a changing church, their belief that they will grow and mature.

Recently some farmers in our area have begun to grow food for the homeless and hungry. They plant extra acres of corn and potatoes in the spring, make arrangements with a food gleaning network for the harvesting of the vegetables, have congregations pick the food, and have it distributed through shelters and food pantries. They are literally sowing seeds of faith. Living plants become symbols of the faith of the congregation that is able to see beyond itself and believe in a future beyond itself. The congregation that moves beyond itself is moving outward toward inclusion.

Sowing Hope

To proclaim hope is to name it. As a pastor you have a powerful ministry in articulating the hope you see and feel in your own spirit. You also have a powerful ministry in leadership in helping your people to proclaim the hope they see and feel within the church. When we see the word *hope* in the Bible, it is used more often as a noun than as a verb. Hope is something we *have* as opposed to something we *do*. Hope is always focused on the future. It signals an opening of the future to the wonder of God's transforming presence. It has to do with believing in what is yet to come. It leads to ordering the life of the congregation around goals that become programs that are seeds of hope.

A small membership church used its original building for more than a century. A couple who worshiped there tragically lost a daughter. At that time the church was in decline and worship was conducted in its old decaying building. The church had a cemetery beside it. The young couple could not bring themselves to bury their daughter in the shadow of a dying church. The man had a vision of a church that could be built to serve and attract the surrounding community. He began to draw up plans and consult the members, the pastor, and denominational leaders. The church did not really have enough active members to support the project yet the administrative council held an open meeting and invited all interested people to attend to consider the new building. So many people came that there was not enough seating available. People stood around the walls and sat in the open windows. The man presented his proposal. After much discussion there was a vote. Only six people voted to build the new church. Fortunately, *no* people voted against it. With only the faith and hope of those six people the church began a building project. Within two years the new building was built, dedicated, paid for, and filled with worshipers. Half a century later the building is still a thriving and growing small membership church with around eighty people in attendance every Sunday.

Not all building projects go so well. Another church was adding an educational wing to its structure. There was a spirit of dissension and conflict. The pastor called upon the church council to stop the project and have the entire church enter a period of prayer and fasting until they could discern God's will for their future. After two months of reflection they moved ahead with their building plans. The two months were necessary for the members to be able to come together with a vision of what God wanted them to do in their future. The addition was finally built with the support of the congregation.

Proclaiming visions of what we discern as God's will for the church shapes the hope of others. Laypeople and clergy alike are sensitive to the needs of the community around the church and are sensitive to the winds of God's spirit moving through the community. Proclamation sows seed of hope.

Sowing Love

God is love. Jesus gave his disciples a new commandment—that they love one another with the same love that he had for them. The church is a place of nurture in which people learn to love. The greatest strategies for inclusion are about love.

A young pastor moved into a small town and began to develop a congregation. At first they worshiped as a home church. With only a few families they began to move from home to home. As they grew they soon became so large that they no longer fit into the home of any of the members. The pastor looked around the community. When he walked down the street many young people would stop their playing and come over to touch him and talk with him. One day he looked down the block and saw the town's liquor store. He saw a lot of the young children hanging around it and playing in the street in front of it. He saw many young adults coming and going from the liquor store. He walked to the liquor store and stood in front of it. He looked across the street and saw a vacant building for sale. The pastor began to feel that God wanted the new congregation to meet there. The members agreed, and in several weeks they bought the property and began their life across the street from the liquor store and on the block where children played in the street. A love for children led the pastor and the church to sow the seed of love in the fertile ground of the small town's streets.

A church in a small community has decided to sow the seed of love in their town by picking different streets and praying for the people who live on that street every day. The pastor told me that she and the members go from one street to the next. They do this praying from their homes and schools and offices. They do it together in prayer meetings and in their own devotions at home. They place cards on the doorknobs telling the residents that they are praying for them. The pastor says that these prayers have resulted in a deeper sensitivity to the spiritual life of the community on the part of the church.

Love grows where it is sown. Love transforms. It gives faith to those in despair. It gives hope to those who suffer. Your community needs transforming love. Your church will bring that love. Before they can give it they need to receive it. You need that love also. Before you give it you need to receive it. God is already pouring that love into you and into your church. God is also pouring that love into the community where you serve. As a pastor you can lead your people in sowing.

Our local ministerial association is currently working on plans for an extended parish for inclusion and hospitality. It is to be made up of members of all interested congregations in the area. Initially we will meet for monthly Sunday afternoon worship and a shared fellowship meal. Location will rotate between participating churches. This initiative is an outgrowth of an annual Lenten series that began here many years ago. The program involved midweek worship services during Lent. Each service was followed by a fellowship meal served by the host church. Care was taken to rotate between African American and white churches. African American pastors always spoke at white churches, and white pastors always spoke at African American churches. Both the clergy and the people enjoyed the worship and fellowship so much that the attendance grew until each service attracted a capacity crowd for the church. Longing to continue the spirit of inclusion that the services fostered, concerned clergy and laity began to talk about expanding the program. As an outgrowth of the above services an interracial support group began meeting monthly. The purpose of the group was to pray and share concerns around issues of interracial harmony and inclusion. We meet for one and a half hours once a month. We have also all set aside one day a week for prayer and fasting.

One all-white small membership church in our area has recently hired an African American associate pastor. His role is evangelism in the African American and Mexican communities and education in the white church. This ministry began because the pastor, his wife, and some of the members shared a vision of their church ministering to people of color in the community because it was what they felt God was calling them to do. The ministry is going well.

One of the small membership churches nearby has entered into a partnership with a church of a different ethnic background. The churches are sponsoring a joint Vacation Bible School. Many of the children involved are already friends from school. This program is focusing on inclusion and hospitality from within the educational program of the church.

The missions committee of one small church has decided to ask the church for a large sum of money. The money is used to support missions at the discretion of the committee. They prayerfully consider local, national, and international needs, and seek to discern how God wants them to act and spend their funds. An effort is made to support both local and global need. Some of the funds go to the family of a child with disabilities. Some of the money goes to support a missionary that the church has a covenant relationship with. The relationship involves pledging money and prayers to the missionary. Some of the money is used to adopt a needy local family. These funds go toward buying clothes, school supplies, and Christmas gifts. By sowing these seed of love the committee is able to see the result of some of their work. They also learn more about how God works through them to touch the needy of their community and their world.

One small church has a very enthusiastic evangelism committee. The chair of that committee is a woman who loves God and people. She has led the committee to begin a card-writing campaign. Cards are written to members when they miss church or when they are sick. She also takes tapes of our worship services and our bulletins to the local nursing home and assisted living facility where some of our members live. Evangelism is about spreading the good news of God's love. By taking the good news to people through cards, visits, and tapes of our services this dear sister is sowing the seed of God's love. She is showing the people of the church that they are cared about.

I once pastored a church with more than fifty members who were homebound. One woman, Janie, was confined to her bedroom, yet she used the phone a lot. I helped her and several other homebound members to form a phone ministry with each other. Each day several of them would call one another in the spirit of God's love to talk and share their journey. In so doing they were sowing the seed of God's love. Even the smallest church has members like Janie who can still help sow the seed of God's love.

Sometimes members are skeptical when the pastor comes to them with ideas of how they can grow spiritually. One of my mentors taught me that it is always best to approach any situation from several angles. When I arrived at a small, rural pastoral appointment I discovered three small churches that hardly knew that they were connected in any way other than sharing a pastor. I began to use prayer concerns time in worship to mention prayer concerns from the other two churches. If a member of one church was sick I would mention that person in the other churches. If there was a training or fellowship event going on in one of the churches I would mention it to the other two. Over time two of the churches decided to have a joint Bible study. It has been going on successfully for several years now. What really overcame the roadblocks were the people. One of the elders of one of the churches was in the hospital and received a visit from a member of one of the other churches. The member had driven sixty miles to make the visit. He simply walked into the room and said, "I'm sorry to hear you've been sick. I just wanted you to know that we are remembering you in our prayers." Later that elder of the church came to me and said, "I didn't want to discourage you when you said we could do things together between churches. I've seen other pastors try it and it never worked, but you have made it work by bringing the other church into our prayers and our life."

Credit for that does not really belong to me. It belongs to the body of Christ. On this spiritual journey all of our small membership churches are called upon to sow God's seed of love. When we sow seed we are participating in the life of God. The life of God is healing and redemptive. It brings people together. It brings people to God in a conscious way.

The small membership church has a special place in the life of the church. Indeed, it has a special place in the life of God. The small church I came from has produced three pastors and one pastor's wife during the last fifty years. The small churches I now serve have produced four pastors during the last fifty years. In this small, rural district of The United Methodist Church, about a third of our clergy are women and men who have come out of our small rural churches. Aside from that these churches have produced generations of people who have grown up to be teachers, nurses, farmers, lawyers, and people of almost every profession. They have produced Christians who have been nurtured in the faith and who have gone on to various leadership positions in the church and the world. I end this book with the prayer and wish that each of you will come to know the presence of God in yourselves and in your churches. May that presence lead to a sense of integrity and inclusion. May it lead you to become the pastors and churches God calls you to be.